THE LAST *of the* MARKET HUNTERS

THE LAST
OF THE MARKET
HUNTERS

By DALE HAMM

With DAVID BAKKE

SOUTHERN ILLINOIS UNIVERSITY PRESS

Carbondale and Edwardsville

11 10 09 08   4 3 2 1

Illustrations on title page and chapter openings by T. M. Shortt.
Copyright © 1996, 2008 by T. M. Shortt.

Library of Congress Cataloging-in-Publication Data
Hamm, Dale, 1916–
     The last of the market hunters / by Dale Hamm, with David Bakke.
         p.   cm.
     1. Hamm, Dale, 1916–. 2. Hunters—United States—Biography.
3. Waterfowl shooting—Illinois—Illinois River. I. Bakke, David, 1951–.
II. Title.
SK17.H285A3   1996
639.1'092—dc20   96-13329
[B]   CIP
ISBN 0-8093-2075-4 (alk. paper)
ISBN 0-8093-2076-2 (pbk. : alk. paper)
ISBN 978-0-8093-2075-2 (alk. paper)
ISBN 978-0-8093-2076-9 (pbk. : alk. paper)

The paper used in this publication meets the minimum requirements of
American National Standard for Information Sciences—Permanence of
Paper for Printed Library Materials, ANSI Z39.48-1992. ⊖

CONTENTS

FOREWORD

I hunt ducks near a small town in Illinois called Bath. I hunt at a place called Grand Island and have for the past thirty-four years. A very famous duck hunter named Van Campen Heilner once said, "When all the ducks are gone, there will still be mallards on the Illinois River."

Grand Island is a natural island around which the Illinois River flows. It seems like the type of place Heilner had in mind.

In the fall, after the natural duck foods have matured, the island is flooded, making it an attractive place for waterfowl. In the spring, after the birds have completed their northern migration, the water is drained from the marsh allowing vegetation to grow and become ideal habitat.

There are about five thousand acres of timber and marsh on Grand Island. In high-water years, it offers magnificent timber shooting for birds returning from the adjacent cornfields.

The Grand Island Hunting Club is privately owned. It was founded in 1902 strictly for the purpose of duck hunting. My grandfather, father, and now my son have all hunted there. I enjoy it with a passion. I love to hunt ducks, have since I was a child, and will until I am unable to put on a pair of hip boots.

There is a man called Dale Hamm who is a legend in this area. He and I are both duck hunters, but his story is different from mine. In his youth, Dale hunted as a matter of survival. He developed skills and knowledge that are now scarce on the waterfowl scene because of the shorter seasons and very small bag limits. Dale's career included the taking of ducks, both legally and illegally. He was a guide for others, a market gunner, and a poacher. Though we've never hunted together, I suspect he excelled in all these areas. That's all behind him now, but he still hunts for pleasure and has never lost the thrill or excitement that comes from being on a marsh where there are ducks, dogs, and decoys. Had our circumstances been reversed, Dale might be writing this foreword, and I might be the one telling a story such as his in this book.

I first heard about Dale when I was hunting with Pot Clark, who lives in Bath, and Bill Drake. We were enjoying a hunt in a little timber hole on the club. The ducks were coming off the south end of the lake and flying over the timber. They'd circle several times and then drop into our decoys. We were enjoying our hunt when, suddenly, there was a barrage of shots followed by a virtual cloud of ducks rising below us.

"Who is that?" I asked. To my knowledge, there was no one else hunting that day.

Pot and Bill knew immediately who it was that day, and who had been hunting that marsh for years before I ever did.

"Oh," they said, "that's just Dale Hamm and some of his friends."

Over the years, that scene has been repeated many times. Though I'm certain there were other local characters involved, Dale, with his reputation, was always high on the list of suspects.

Long after meeting Dale, whom I enjoyed immediately, I

would encounter him near the river and would be amazed that he always knew where the ducks were on our island. In fact, I often selected my blind for a morning's hunt based on Dale's up-to-the-minute reconnaissance of the area.

Dale Hamm is a legend among many of the local hunters—many of whom deserve the same title. He baffled and dodged the many watchmen our club hired to catch him. But over the years, those of us who have come to know him have grown rather fond of him. I doubt that he will ever be offered an honorary membership at the Grand Island Duck Club, but he knows the territory better than most of the members. And he has enjoyed hunting there longer than any of us. After reading his story, you've got to love it and admire his successes.

Dale has a unique story to tell. Thanks, from those of us who will read *The Last of the Market Hunters*. We'll see you in the fall.

Barney Donnelly

ACKNOWLEDGMENT**S**

Grateful acknowledgment is made to the *State Journal-Regis-ter* (Springfield, Illinois) to reprint the introduction, which originally appeared in *Heartland,* © 1991 the *State Journal-Register,* as "Land of the Duck." For their stories in the section "Lore, Legends, and Lies," we thank the following: Dale's daughters, Sue Tarvin and Marilyn Ford, and his sons, Ron and Don; Leo Curless; New York Mets pitcher Mark Clark; John E. Fletcher; Harold (Itze) Ellsworth; Bob (Lobo) Lane; *International Game Warden* publisher Don Hastings (former head of undercover operations for the then Illinois Depart-ment of Conservation, now the Illinois Department of Nat-ural Resources); Tom Flattery of the Illinois Department of Natural Resources; Ernie Hoff; Dee Willard; and Bernice Oest.

INTRODUCTION

I t begins well before dawn, with two white lights coming through the darkness, then the rushing wind of a passing car, then two red pinpoints of light disappearing into the night. The highway is unusually busy for so early in the morning.

This is Illinois Highway 78 in November. It has been busy every duck-hunting season since the turn of the century. Since before there were cars. When the skies were black with ducks.

This annual rite has enriched the lore and color of Duck Alley a hundredfold. The lure of the cards and the dice and the ducks brought the rich from Chicago to rub elbows with the river rats.

Seventy-eight from Virginia to Havana passes by Matanza Beach and Wimpyville through Quiver Beach and Bath, a half block from Dale Hamm's trailer home. It goes past Marvin Adams's Discount Sales, the Brick Tavern, the County Line Restaurant, and the ashes of the Duck Inn. Seventy-eight is the road of legends like Hamm, Baseball-Hall-of-Famer Marty Marion, and Bigfoot.

If not for the duck, this would be just another stretch of road, quiet and cold in the predawn hours. But, then, that's not quite true, either.

"It's the worst damn road in the state," says County Line co-owner Doug Gerdes.

Thirty mallards in thirty minutes. Five thousand six hundred seventy ducks killed at one hunting club in one year. Eight hundred sixty-seven in one day. Those numbers make the modern hunter want to throw his shotgun in the fireplace, take up knitting, and rue the luck of being born too late.

But that's the way it was in the early 1900s. When a drainage canal raised the Illinois River south of Peoria four feet, it created marshy wetlands along its length. In other words, duck heaven.

In 1902, four men created the Sanganois Club, the first duck-hunting club near the confluence of the Illinois and Sangamon Rivers. A hunting record of the club founder, Ralph Hobart, still exists, covering 1895 to 1949. His detailed entries speak volumes about himself and the ducks—166 mallards in five days, a limit taken in half an hour, and limits declining over the years from 50 to 25 to 10 and then 4.

A day in 1901 at Crane Lake, seven miles west of 78, changed duck hunting forever. That day, four men killed 867 ducks. The next year, in large part owing to that day, the first duck limits were established in the United States. The limit was 50 a day.

In 1948, the state of Illinois bought the land that included the Sanganois Club. Since then, the state has operated the 9,700-acre Sanganois Conservation Area, with public hunting on the site.

Gary Senn was the site superintendent for sixteen years, until 1992. He and four Department of Conservation (which in 1996 became the Department of Natural Resources) employees tended the Sanganois. It's easy to get lost in its twisting narrow chutes, sloughs, and swales.

"It took me five years of being out here every day to really figure out how it all works," Senn said. "We've had people get lost out there. Somebody usually ends up finding them somewhere."

People have reported seeing mountain lions and bears ("Probably black labs," snorts Senn), and there was one Bigfoot sighting reported. That turned out to be a practical joke, but Senn says he can almost believe it.

"I've had my vehicle break down out there at three or four in the morning," he says. "I've heard sounds like I've never heard before."

The glory days of hunting are gone, thanks to man and the weather. Drought in Canada's breeding grounds has cut the duck population. Farming practices and silting have filled in wetlands.

Senn quit hunting years ago. He retired after the 1992 season.

"I got second thoughts about running a duck club," he said. "I see those dead ducks lying there and I wonder if it's worth it. I guess that's why a lot of the older guys have quit now. That and the dwindling population. But I had my years when nothing was too rough. I'd be out there."

Six-foot-two is big for a shortstop, but that was Marty Marion. Marion played for the St. Louis Cardinals from 1940 to 1953, including four World Series appearances.

He found Duck Alley in the 1940s, courtesy of Ellis Breech, an East St. Louis sportswriter.

"Breech would invite [Enos] Slaughter, [Stan] Musial, and Red Schoendienst and me to a place called the Lakewood Club in Bath," says Marion. "We'd hunt ducks and stay at the Lakewood. Being an old baseball player, you get to know a lot of people. I got to know a guy at Chain Lake and I kept coming up every year. I ended up buying three places of my own."

Those were the years of the black skies—when shooting a limit of ducks was common.

"I could see every year it was getting worse," says Marion. He finally quit hunting and sold his club and house to the state in 1987. It became part of the Sanganois.

But Marion stayed in Duck Alley, building a house near Chandlerville. Opening day of duck season finds him gazing out his window at cold, gray skies and remembering what a friend of his once said.

"He always said these cold and windy days are the best for ducks," Marion says. "I miss it. I loved it, but I had my time."

About noon on opening day, the hunters start coming into the County Line Restaurant. It's the oldest tavern in Mason County. The decor is definitely duck. There's a duck saw, a chalk drawing of ducks, a duck calendar, duck decoys, and mallard place mats. The soup of the day is chili. The style of the day is camouflage.

"A lot of hunters come in here after they've fallen out of their boats," says co-owner Kay Gerdes. "And they'll hold their ducks up outside so we can look at them. Sometimes we fry hamburgers for their dogs."

Dale Hamm comes in and it's as if one of the Beatles stopped by. People talk to him, try to set up hunts with him. They know his outlaw reputation, but that only makes him all the more popular here.

Hamm is somewhat respectable now. He mended fences with most of the private club owners he once tormented. Among his regular hunting partners is Itze Ellsworth, the only man ever to be sheriff of two different counties—Fulton and Cass—in Illinois.

He has a story about Hamm, as most everyone does. His is that Hamm had been caught doing something or other that was illegal and had his hunting license suspended for one year. He couldn't stand not hunting and couldn't let a technicality like no license stop him. So he went out with Ellsworth, who brought along an extra shotgun.

Introduction

"Then," says Ellsworth, "I got a call from a federal judge who said I'd better stop hunting with Dale because the heat was coming down."

Ellsworth, being sheriff of Cass County at the time, appreciated the tip. He went on to become assistant director of the Illinois Department of Conservation.

Marvin Adams says he and Dale "have been arguing for sixty years." Adams's Discount Sales is right on Highway 78 in Matanza.

Discount Sales looks as if someone opened the door, threw a hand grenade inside, and then closed the door. It has a disorderly orderliness to it—hunting supplies here, beer over there. Or at least it did until the state made him stop selling beer and guns both. He kept the guns and got rid of the beer.

Before opening Discount Sales in 1961, Adams ran a casino in Matanza Beach. When gambling was wide open along Highway 78, it lured Al Capone down from Chicago to kill some ducks and gamble.

"Then," says Adams, "the police raided twenty-three places in the county. We were raided on Halloween night. I thought it was a joke—somebody'd dressed up for Halloween. The guy said 'This is no joke. It's a raid.'"

Adams's brother, Corbert, was a state policeman, so Marvin figured it might help to mention that. Maybe he could get a break.

"Heck," a patrolman answered, "Corbert Adams is in charge of this raid."

Marvin once belonged to Snicarte Lodge Gun Club. *Snicarte* is French for "narrow channel." This stretch of Highway 78 has an odd mix of foreign influences. Havana shares its name with the Cuban capital. Matanzas with an *s* is another Cuban city. Bath is a city in England.

Snicarte Lodge is one of the many private hunting clubs that dot the Illinois River. Some clubs are the province of the

Chicago rich that Dale resents. Other clubs simply have large numbers of owners, thus making it affordable for the non-rich.

Adams is another hunter who eventually quit. His Discount Sales entryway is a sort of community billboard. Signs sell puppies and taxidermy services and tell people where to report badger sightings. Adams calls it the "Chinese Wall."

Another of those curious foreign influences.

At the north end of Highway 78 is Havana, home of the Ducks. Havana High School's teams have been known as the Ducks since 1924.

"The whole town has always been duck-hunting oriented," says the school's athletic director Dick Lounsberry. "When duck season came in, everybody went out the door—the kids and the teachers. The football players would skip practice to go hunting."

The football team was so duck daffy it once stopped during a game to watch flocks of ducks fly overhead. Players broke out of the huddle, headed for the line of scrimmage, and ended up just staring at the sky.

David Bakke

THE LAST *of the* MARKET HUNTERS

O N E

They call me an outlaw and a renegade, a man who would rather take somebody else's game than eat. That's not exactly right. The fact is, I would rather take somebody else's game than starve.

They call us outlaws, poachers. But that's the name the federal and state game wardens gave us. To us, it was a way of life. It was the way we've always made our living, in any season or in any way we could do it just to keep bread and butter on the table.

My dad, Pete, and my mother, Maye, had eight children: six boys—me, Dallas, J. C., Marshall, Pete Jr., and Virgil—and two girls, Wanda and Glenna. I was the third oldest.

Back when my brothers and I were growing up in the 1930s, there was very little cash. The fish we caught sold for a half-cent a pound. Our cash, what we didn't make from fishing, came from market hunting. Some call it poaching. It was the Illinois River version of running moonshine. Only we ran ducks. And we were good at it.

My family made its living by the net and the gun and the traps.

As a kid living along the Illinois River north of Beardstown, I used to follow my dad around on the river. My family made its living by the net and the gun and the traps. We didn't have a car back in the 1930s, so we walked to the river and went by boat from there, sometimes hunting all night before coming back the next day. A lot of times we would go on the river during daylight and climb trees to take raccoons out to sell them for groceries. We hunted what we could hunt, and we ate what we could eat. The rest we sold for things we didn't have the money to buy. That was our way of life.

I was born in Bluff City, at home, in 1916. Mom had all the kids at home as far as I can remember. My dad farmed in his younger days. I'd go hunting with him even when I was too young to hold a gun. I'd just sit in the blind when he took the hunters out.

Dad always kept us in line. He was the kind of dad we ought to have today. I ran from him one time and that took care of that. He caught me because he could outrun me. He was a good ballplayer, a good pitcher for the Bluff City team. The fact is he could have been a big-leaguer if he'd gone ahead with it. His dad tried to get him to go but he wouldn't. They couldn't beat him around here, playing baseball. Dad died in 1974 and he was seventy-four years old. My mom died a few years ago at age ninety-three.

I went to school through the eighth grade and one day of high school. My dad couldn't afford to send me to school anymore. I had been out of school a couple of years, and the principal of Browning High School wanted me to play baseball. I was a fairly good baseball player. They said they'd give me a scholarship if I'd come back and play ball. I went one day and was so out of place because I was older than the other kids that I had to get out of there.

After that, I hunted and fished with my dad until I was seventeen. Then I went to Macomb to a hemp factory and worked. One of the duck hunters was a boss there and got me a job. I worked at the hemp factory for a short time but got homesick and quit. Then it was back to hunting for a living. That was our life.

I guided at Anderson Lake for quite a few years. It was a private club. I started pushing (guiding) there when I was fourteen or fifteen. They paid me a salary and I got tips.

We hunted what we could hunt, and we ate what we could eat. The rest we sold for things we didn't have the money to buy. That was our way of life.

Market Hunters

I remember Billy Einfeld, an old man I got paired up with, was hesitant about such a young kid taking him hunting. After I got out there with him, we got our ducks before anyone else. So every time after that, he said he'd give me a couple extra dollars if we got our ducks first. Most of the time we'd be out of there ahead of the other hunters. I pushed for the old man for a lot of years.

He's the type we worked for and sold to. We didn't make a lot of money, but for the way we lived, it was enough. Dad and us boys would kill two hundred ducks in just a few shots. You've seen pictures of ducks so thick they were touching each other? That's the way they were. That was terrible to shoot into them like that but we did it, we don't deny it. We're not proud of it, either. It was back in the Depression when even the millionaires couldn't afford to come to their own hunting clubs. Some gave their clubs up because they couldn't afford it.

When you market hunt, you need a place to dispose of the game. Obviously, a family like ours that lived by its fishing tackle and guns didn't sell game to other families of the same kind because they had plenty of their own and were also looking for places to sell game. It was the city sportsmen and businessmen who decided the surplus fish and ducks would make a special dish for their friends and customers. That's who we sold to.

Because of the price the high-class people would pay, the market hunter couldn't resist. We'd break the law, get all the ducks we could, and try to make things better for our families by selling them. It was better than robbing or stealing.

To stop us, the government spent the taxpayers' money to hire more game wardens. They arrested the rivermen who were only trying to make a living for their families. But as time went on, the poor warden found himself in trouble because he also caught some of those wealthy sportsmen who bought large tracts of land and went about the business of violating the law on their own property.

What that meant for the warden was that he got fired. The message for their replacements was clear: arrest all the rivermen you want but leave the wealthy gun clubs alone.

When the rivermen found out about the double standard, we figured we could cheat a little too. Pretty soon, the numbers of hunters increased, and they began to poach on the big clubs. The money boys didn't appreciate that very much. At first, they tried chasing the hunters away, even resorting to shooting some of them. But that didn't help. It only made the rivermen more determined and angry.

Over the years, the rivermen learned that the clubs were illegally hand-feeding corn to their large numbers of ducks. They also found different species of ducks that had been shot and wasted because the big sportsmen only wanted the sport, not the ducks. If it wasn't a mallard drake, they wouldn't bother to pick it up. When I was guiding for them and I'd go out to pick up the ducks, I'd stick the little ducks in a muskrat house. Whenever we were done hunting, I'd go back out there and get my ducks.

In at least one case, some members of one club had been hitting the bottle pretty good when they caught some hunters trespassing and came up with a new idea for getting rid of poachers. They tossed about twenty teal ducks into one of the hunters' boats, then told them to get out and stay out. If they happened to get stopped by a warden on the way back, with those twenty ducks in the boat, they'd be in a hell of a mess.

Because of the friction between the rivermen and the local game wardens, the feds stepped in. And ran into the Hamms.

If anybody ever cut a chunk out of any of us Hamm boys, it probably would have tasted like fish or duck. We didn't have the money to go to the grocery store. If we wanted groceries, we had to go out in the woods and shoot ducks or catch fish. We bought bread and cornmeal, and that was the extent of what we could afford.

We didn't have much, but we did have the Illinois River.

All of us felt the river was put here to give people something to eat. We were raised that way, and our Dad taught us all we knew about the river. It was born and bred in us. We're not alone. There are thousands like us, who either have made or are trying to make a living doing the things I have done all my life. We are a vanishing breed and, like the Indians who preceded us along the river, speak with a small voice compared with politicians and other self-righteous people who tried to deprive us of a way to make a living and from enjoying a way of life.

People got bitter with us Hamm boys, because most of them owned the land we poached on. We couldn't afford to buy land, so we would sneak onto theirs and take their game and they'd get a little mad at us.

The fish and ducks were put there for everybody. There was no reason for them to get mad. We were going to get some of what they had, no matter what they did, no matter what laws they made.

I have always felt a strong kinship with the Indians who lived along the river for thousands of years before us. A lot of people are beginning to agree with me that the Indians were noble people. White people used to call them savages, and worse. The Indians, though, started it all. They knew what they were doing. It makes me mad as hell that we forced the Indian out and took over. What's almost as bad is that the politicians pushed the rest of us out and took control themselves. They had help from powerful commercial interests. They told us, "You can't make a living on that river. We don't want you to." To excuse what they did, they said they were going to use the river for sportsmen. Who could find fault with that? I can't. I want people to enjoy the river. That is why it's there. I think it should be for people whoever they are, not just the rich who own companies or buy up big chunks of land where ducks have been landing and feeding for thousands of years.

I have always felt a strong kinship with the Indians who lived along the river for thousands of years before us.

Everybody loves the river. They fish in it. They hunt along it, and they run and up and down on it in high-powered boats. They also find a good deal of solitude in it, sitting along its banks, watching the water flow quietly by, bringing some dreams with it.

When he was a surveyor, Abraham Lincoln laid out the town of Bath, which is where I live now. It's only a few hundred people, four taverns, and the Bath Chute, which is a waterway that runs into the Illinois River.

In Lincoln's time, this area was the pride of the Illinois. Everybody wanted to go to the Illinois River. Hell, they still do. You can see them down there now, wading in the mud to get to the water. That's the way it is. The river has become one big ditch. Some people don't see it as a place for recreation or enjoyment, they see it as a highway on which to move products in barges from one place to another.

They built levees along its banks on both sides, forcing what was once a wide, shallow river into a deeper, faster-flowing stream, filled with silt and other debris. Farmers plow their hillsides and the water runoff carries silt into the lakes. The silt drops to the bottom, filling up the lakes and destroying a natural wildlife paradise.

We've always had silt. But the levees are something else again. In the old days, lakes and marshes stretched out on either side of the river. providing a natural floodplain when the rains came. Of course, people who farmed along the river complained about that, so up went the levees and those floodplains became farmland.

The river has been squeezed up like a fat lady in an old-fashioned corset. So when the corset breaks, the water spreads out like all that blubber. It amazes me that people are surprised when a levee breaks. It's just the river taking back its own.

We love this river because it is the last source of natural pleasure we have. It's something that can't be replaced. The

Indians believed that no one person can own the land. They figured it was for everybody, and that the game on the land belonged to everybody. They didn't have a bad idea.

Market hunting has dried up, and we're too old to run from the game wardens anymore. But when we did, we'd get our asses hung for trespassing to kill a deer. We'd get punished quicker and more severely than a narcotics dealer. We were treated like criminals, while the dope peddlers slid through, getting their hands slapped. But for us, it was always, "We'll put them in jail. We'll make an example of the Hamm boys."

We've got reason to be bitter, though we don't have any more right to be bitter than the rest of the people along this river. It took a hell of a long time to mess up paradise.

T W O

Back in the middle 1930s, the Sanganois Conservation Area was the place for locals to hunt ducks. During the Depression, the private gun clubs gave it up and opened it to the rest of us.

My father, Pete, and all of my brothers hunted it. It was a duck hunter's paradise—lots of ducks and few hunters. It was, and still is, one of the best places in the country for duck hunting. Anybody who thinks they can go into the Sanganois and get right back out is wrong. I hear so many of them say, "I wouldn't have any trouble, I know my directions."

Well, they can know all the directions they want to know, but when they go in there, they are not going to come out on their own unless it's an accident. There's too many sloughs, and you've got to go around them. You think you're going to take a compass and go north, but when you come to one of those sloughs, which way are you going to go? I got lost for two days in there.

I was about eighteen years old and was with my kid brother Marshall, who was ten. I thought I knew the Sanganois like my dad did because I followed him for so many years. But I found out I didn't know it so well, because my brother and I ventured in there coon hunting and got lost.

We were climbing trees and punching the coons out or shooting them in the tree, then skinning the hides out. It was in December, very cold. Instead of going in from the Browning side, which we were familiar with, we went in from the east side. We crossed a big drift where logs had piled up and dammed the Sangamon River. The water had raised after we got in there. We hunted all day long, so when we started home, we couldn't cross places where we'd gone in because of the higher water.

I changed my route, got lost and started walking in circles. I saw some people going down the lake toward Browning and I hollered at them, but they couldn't hear me because their motor was running. I could hear the geese on Knapp Island so I knew which direction that was, but we couldn't get across the sloughs to get there. It came dark on us, so we built a fire. It was lucky we had matches because neither one of us smoked.

We stretched the coon hides out and Marshall slept on them. I stayed up all night making sure the fire didn't go out. The next morning we started out. When Marshall got worn out, I tried to carry him but couldn't make it. We just walked in a circle and came right back to our fire. After a while, at nine or ten o'clock, some fishermen came to raise their nets in a slough we were by. So we asked them to tell us which way to go to get back to that big logjam.

When Marshall got worn out, I tried to carry him but couldn't make it. We just walked in a circle and came right back to our fire.

They said to follow the slough we were on and we'd come to it. We wanted to get to the logjam and walk across the logs to the other side. My dad had been hunting for us all night and as we went up the slough, we could hear him hollering. He was tickled to death to find us. My mother thought I'd fallen out of a tree and gotten hurt or maybe even killed my damn self, and that kid with me wouldn't know what to do.

Instead of going to the logs and crossing the river to my

car, we walked with him to his boat and went home that way. A fella named Roy Sherril went back to get my car, got stuck in the sand, and broke an axle on it.

While we were lost, I never seemed to get scared. Maybe Marshall was, but it didn't seem to bother me. I worried because I couldn't find my way. It was embarrassing more than anything. The Sanganois is a good place to get in trouble, and it's not always because of the difficulty in getting around in there.

Sometimes we would hunt there with the Curless boys— Robert and Jim Sr. and Jim Jr. When we weren't hunting with them, we'd meet them on the way there or on the way back. My mother, Maye, was a Curless, so they were family.

But then Jim Jr. took a job as a game warden. I never will forget when he got that job. I was building a cabin near Anderson Lake. Jim came up while I was working and told me.

I said, "Jim, that's fine, but you should have taken the job in a different area. You know all our hunting spots, and that's not good for us."

Jim told me that just because he knew us, that didn't mean he'd let us go. He couldn't jeopardize his job. I told Jim he was jeopardizing our hunting.

The Curless boys had some land that joined the Sanganois and also joined Oscar Linn's property. We'd come back from the service in the 1940s and started to hunt the Sanganois again. Little did we know that, in the meantime, it had been closed again to public hunting.

J. C. and I decided we'd take some boys out there to hunt. We took Bob Lashbrook who was the sheriff of Schuyler County, Illinois, and my son Ron, who was only about twelve. We found a pile of driftwood we used for a blind. We put out our decoys and got ourselves situated in the driftwood. In a few minutes, the ducks started coming in. We shot the hell out of them and had a great time.

We heard a boat coming, and it eventually pulled up next

to our driftwood. It was Oscar. He said we were trespassing on his property. He had No Trespassing signs posted on the old river, but we were outside the signs and never saw them. He told us to leave. I told him to go to hell, that we'd hunted there all our lives and we weren't going to stop.

Finally, Oscar said he was going to get the law and have us put off the property. I told him he was a son of a bitch, and that he could go ahead but we were not leaving. Oscar left. We continued to kill ducks.

In about an hour we heard another boat coming. Sure enough, it was Oscar. And he had Zeb Kost, the chief game warden, with him. Then we heard a second boat. That one had another game warden and Dale Booth, one of Oscar's caretakers.

Both boats pulled up to our driftwood. That's when things got ugly. I called Oscar a no-good son of a bitch for bringing the warden down on us. The argument got so hot that I started down to his boat to throw him in the river and Zeb along with him. Zeb said, "Don't do it Dale, I can't swim."

About that time, Booth and the second game warden came to help Oscar. I said to Booth, "You big red-headed son of a bitch, you better stay where you are."

About that time, my brother raised up from behind the driftwood. J. C. said, "Go ahead, Dale, toss him in and I'll help you." Booth froze right there.

Finally, I told Oscar that since we couldn't shoot ducks where we were, we'd shoot them a little closer to his club-house. Oscar said that would be fine, it would make it that much easier for him to catch us. I told him he better be careful or he'd stub his toe and shoot himself. He knew what I meant.

When Oscar, Booth, and the game wardens saw we wouldn't back down, they gave up. That's when the wardens decided to ask for our licenses. We were all OK. Except me. I had left my billfold at home.

After I had that run-in with Oscar Linn, I leased quite a bit

He told us to leave. I told him to go to hell, that we'd hunted there all our lives and we weren't going to stop.

of his duck-hunting land from him. After threatening him and everything, he leased it to me, and we got along fine.

Most of the scrapes we got into didn't amount to anything serious. We usually were able to take care of things on our own. But we had a couple of experiences that got out of hand.

In the early '30s my dad, Pete, and my brother Dallas, a friend of ours named Oris Lamb, and I were going out to hunt. It was a cold and snowy night. Dad said it was a good night to hunt ducks on Crane Lake. The lake was frozen solid, but there was always Horn Slough that ran from the Sangamon River into Crane Lake. The slough's current was so swift it helped keep the water open even in subzero weather. It had thousands of ducks sitting on it, and they worked to keep it open.

We had a big, wooden sled with a piano box on top that we hooked to the back of our car. That was what we put our ducks in. Dallas and I rode in that box five or six miles to the river. We crossed the frozen river, walked across Stewart Lake and Crane Lake to Horn Slough, pulling the sled on the ice all the way.

It was dark as hell. My dad thought the ducks were sitting thick in the slough. That fast current kept carrying them into the ice, so they'd fly back up to the open water and drop in again. We could hardly see them, it was so dark. We could sure as hell hear them. Thousands of them. We all fired from the bank into where we thought they were and then laid our guns down and ran to the edge of the slough. The water level had fallen, leaving a sheet of ice on a steep slope. Oris slipped down the ice and into the slough. We thought sure as hell he'd come up under the ice. But he was lucky, he came up in open water.

We pulled him out onto the bank and the minute that cold air hit him, his clothes froze to his body. We built a fire, and

Dad happened to have on two layers of clothes because of the cold. He took off one pair of pants and a shirt and gave them to Oris.

We weren't too far from the Crane Lake Hunting Club's clubhouse. Dad thought he heard someone coming, so he didn't want to pick up our ducks just yet. Dallas and I said we'd go get them anyway. Dad and Oris stayed at the fire while we went after the ducks. Though it was black dark out, we could see a log sticking up in the slough. The ducks we killed had drifted up against it. One of us crawled on the log and began tossing the ducks to shore. We had almost all of them out and started tying them by the necks in bunches. We had five or six bunches to put on the sled and drag home. It was over a hundred ducks.

We picked them all by hand, and then our dad hauled them to Chicago and sold them. Oris survived his close call, and we never did get caught that night. What Dad thought were people walking on the snow were really the crippled ducks trying to get away from the shooting.

Oris was lucky, but my nephew Bob wasn't. He and my cousin James Hamm, Ralph McGinnis, and I left Browning early one morning to hunt on Crane Lake. We went up the Sangamon River to where it empties into the Illinois River, walked over Sand Slough to Crane Lake Hunting Club. That's a private club, but we figured we could get away with it.

When we got there, we split up. Jim Hamm and I went one way, Ralph McGinnis and Bob Hamm went another way. Jim and I put up a makeshift blind on a muskrat house. We were shooting ducks, and I could hear Ralph and Bob shooting, too.

After a while, we heard voices coming from where Bob and Ralph were. Then we heard a shot. Jim and I kept real quiet, because we knew the boys up there had company. But it got very quiet in their direction. Then I heard someone coming our way. We stayed quiet until we could see who it was. It was Ralph, but he was alone. When he got close enough, he shouted to us that someone had shot Bob.

"Is he dead?" I asked.

"No," Ralph said, "but he's bleeding pretty bad and they loaded him in a boat and took him to Crane Lake clubhouse."

Ralph said a Crane Lake guide and a club member came up on them from behind in a duck boat. When Ralph and Bob turned around, the club member told them to drop their guns. Instead of dropping his gun, Bob started to sit in the fork of a tree, and about that time, the guy fired his gun and hit Bob's gun on the underside of the barrel, about six inches down from the muzzle. The shot ricocheted off the barrel and hit Bob in the face.

The Crane Lake members took Bob to the Decatur hospital, which wasn't even the nearest one. He was going to be OK, but his face was shot up pretty bad.

The Crane Lake members took Bob to the Decatur hospital, which wasn't even the nearest one. He was going to be OK, but his face was shot up pretty bad.

That night, I drove with my brothers to Havana to see the sheriff and find out what happened. He didn't give us much information. We asked him to put out a warrant for the club member's arrest, but he wouldn't do it. We got the gun back and showed the sheriff that since the shot hit the underside of the barrel, the gun had to be pointed straight up. That meant Bob wasn't shot in self-defense. If he'd have been pointing the gun at somebody, the shot would have hit the muzzle. The sheriff wasn't impressed. He didn't do a damn thing about it.

About a year and a half later, I was with Virgil Ball on a duck-hunting trip. We were talking about Bob's shooting, and he said that in a case of that kind, Bob had two years to file charges. Right away, I went to Browning where Bob lived and told him about that. I knew an attorney in Peoria, and I took Bob to see him.

When we told the lawyer what had happened, he said Bob had a good case. He agreed to work to get that club member to pay for damages. About two months later, we got a call from the lawyer. He'd arranged a meeting and asked us to come in. He said he had been offered $800 as a settlement.

"Couldn't you at least get $1,000?" I asked him.

"You better take the $800 or you won't get anything," he replied.

"Bob," I said, "it's up to you."

Bob took the $800.

By being dumb and green, I think we got took. The guy who shot him was a millionaire. If we'd have done things right, we could have gotten Bob more money. I think the guy would have paid plenty to have his name kept out of the papers because he shot a guy over a duck.

I never got hurt too bad. I got shot a couple of times, but they were accidents. I did fall out of a tree while hunting mushrooms. I had gone to the Sangamon Bottoms to get some mushrooms with a guy named Delbert Clayton. We got back in the wilderness and came to a slough we wanted to get across. There's a tree leaning clear across the slough. I was going to go across that and come down on the other side. I got way out on the tree and got on the other side.

The tree I was on was in the fork of another tree. I broke that fork off and when I did, down came the tree and I'm on it. When it hit the ground, it knocked me out. I was out. I hit my elbow on the tree, split it wide open, and buried the wood in my elbow. Delbert couldn't walk a log if he wanted to, but when I hit the ground, he ran across a log and got over to where I was at. He didn't know whether I was dead or what. It knocked the wind out of me is what happened.

When I did come out of it, I was OK. But my elbow hurt. I pulled my sleeve up, and he said, "You did cut it a little bit." I said, "How does it look?" He said, "Oh, it's OK." He was goofy. I said, "OK."

So we came back out of there and I was getting sick from loss of blood. We got to a tavern and went in to have a drink. It was hurting like the devil, but I thought, well, there's nothing I can do about it, it just has to hurt. So we had a beer, and I showed my elbow to the guys in the tavern. They said,

"Geez, man, you better go to a doctor and get that sewed up!" Here, I couldn't even see it.

I went to a horse doctor in Havana. A horse doctor, that's just what he was. He worked on me and sewed it up. A couple weeks later, I got an infection in it, and it like to drove me crazy. I had to go to another doctor, and he dug wood out that was just buried in my elbow.

The first time I got shot, Rodney Briney and I and some other guys went out hunting. We took two boats. We pulled into a slough and parked on the bank. These guys in the other boat came behind us. We decided we'd try and kill a deer.

There was a dead hog in that slough. It was cold weather. That hog was lying on the water, frozen. One of the goofy bastards from the other boat pulled up and shot that hog. We were on the opposite side of the water. When he shot, we just turned our heads as fast as we could but we couldn't turn them fast enough. The shot ricocheted off the water. We could hear the shot rattling in the trees. I looked down and saw the whole front of my shirt was covered with blood. I didn't feel anything but when I saw that, I thought, "What the hell's going on here?" I had a pellet right in my chin.

That kind of aggravated me. My brother and I chewed him out pretty good. After it was over, I never thought another thing about it. A few years later, I got to fooling around with my chin, and hell, that shot was still in there. It still is.

A guy named Russ Greer and I went pheasant hunting the last day of the season. We were road hunting. Pretty soon I looked back behind me and there was another car. He was following us.

I said, "Russ, I think that's the game warden. We'll turn the corner here." There was a rooster pheasant standing there, so I popped him, ran out, and picked it up. Then I said, "Now, if he comes around this corner and follows us, then we'll know it's the game warden."

We went up about a mile and he was coming. Then we

turned again and he came behind us. Then I parked, jumped out of the car, and ran across the field. I wanted to make him think I'd shot a pheasant and was running out to get it. The warden came up just so far and stopped way behind us. I went back there to him.

"What the hell are you following us for?" I asked him. "You know this is the last day of the pheasant season and we've got to get some birds."

He said, "Are you road hunting?"

"No, I'm not," I said. "Now we're going to go up here, and there's a road that goes to the left and a road that goes to the right. We're going to the right. You just go to the left, will you?" Right up the road, we went left and he went right.

But we ran onto him again. This time, he had the road blocked. We didn't know what was going on there because we didn't think he was looking for us. The farmers had been complaining about guys shooting on their property. He's higher than we are in the Jeep. He looks down into our Jeep and can see our guns aren't cased, and we're obviously road hunting.

"Dale," he says, "you're going to get in trouble because of these farmers complaining about road hunters, and you guys don't have your guns cased."

So we cased our guns, but when we got back almost to Bath, we got out to shoot a bird. I reached down and had a rifle there in case we saw any rabbits. Our damn dog jumped in the car and when he did, that rifle went off. The bullet hit me right in the forearm, went up the forearm, just missed my elbow, and came out just under my armpit. I never even knew it. Never felt it.

I got out of the car when I heard the gun go off. When I did, I dropped my arm down and the blood poured out of my sleeve. I passed out before we got to the hospital.

We were just lucky I had enough gas to get to the hospital. That was my closest shave.

T H R E E

Whom you hear people talk about being in a particular line of work "all their lives," they don't mean that literally. What they mean is that they have been doing something all of their adult lives.

But when I say I've been hunting all my life, I mean just that. My brothers and I have been hunters as long as we can remember. Believe me, those memories run deep.

I can remember back to the 1920s when the hunting was tremendous. I was just a little kid then, having been born in 1916, but I remember a lot of what happened then because it had a profound effect on the rest of my life.

I am told that from the time I could crawl on the ice-cold floor of our home, I would manage to find the corner where my Dad put his hunting coat. I'd dig around in the pockets until I came up with his duck call. Then I would sit there on the floor and drive everyone nuts while I tooted on the damned thing.

In a way, it's funny how my life has gone. The river has been my life, yet it was the river that changed it from being something else.

Market Hunters

My grandfather, Pete Hamm Sr., was a very aggressive farmer and builder. He built most of the town of Sheldon Grove and, in the process, built a home and farm for each of his four sons. He and his sons managed to clear several hundred acres of Kelly Lake drainage area and built the first levees around it. They did it with the ax, the saw, and the horse. It was a job any man would be proud to have accomplished.

They farmed that land until 1926 or 1927. That's when the river entered their lives, and mine. One year, the swollen river broke through the levees and wiped out their corn crop—everything they had was suddenly gone.

We children got up the next morning after the levees broke and saw all the water. To us, it was exciting. But to my father and grandfather, it was the end. They'd seen their hopes and dreams wiped out while they stood by, helpless.

That fall, the ducks started coming. I couldn't guess now how many ducks there were. But from that time on, ducks, fish, and other wild animals became the livelihood of the Hamm family. In season and out of season. We saw nothing wrong with it. It was meat on the table, and we got it any way we could.

Poor people couldn't afford to eat ducks in those days, but the rich could and that's how we established our market. We took a lot of ducks back then.

We'd carry as high as 20 ducks at one time on our shoulder. There'd be a strap over our shoulder, and there'd be 10 on one half of the string and 10 on the back half. We had limits of 15, 12, and 10 a day. One time back in the Depression, though, we had a limit of only 1 duck, and you couldn't shoot any wood ducks. We didn't have Ducks Unlimited at that time, and it was dry weather and the breeding grounds dried up. When Ducks Unlimited got in, they started keeping water in these marshes.

Between hunting ducks, fishing, and shooting raccoons, we got by. We'd get those coons out of the trees without a

Poor people couldn't afford to eat ducks in those days, but the rich could and that's how we established our market. We took a lot of ducks back then.

dog. We'd get a better price for coonskins in the Depression, since the price was better than it is now. We got as high as $15 to $18 for coon; mink was $35 to $40. We were living high compared with our neighbors.

Our neighbors, Bill and Bessie Boyd, lived at a place called Sharpe's Landing, on the river across from Stewart Lake. My grandfather used to drive his livestock there to load them on river packets for shipment to the St. Louis markets. My dad and other hunters also kept their boats there.

One morning, my dad went after his boat and it wasn't there. He searched for it and found it—sunk in the river with the bottom full of holes.

He was more than a little upset when he headed back to Sheldon Grove. One of the first people he saw on the street was Bill Boyd. I don't know why Dad headed straight for Bill. There must have been something that had happened between them. Dad was never very talkative and he didn't have much to say that day, either. He just grabbed Bill by the throat and put him on the ground, choked him until his tongue hung out, and asked him who sank his boat.

Bill couldn't talk very well at that moment but finally managed to whisper that his wife, Bessie, had done it. My grandfather was there, too, and he pulled Dad off Bill, or the story might have had a tragic ending.

A few days later, Bill went to Sheldon Grove for supplies. My Dad's nephew Johnny spotted him. Johnny had already had a nip or two. He ran up to Bill's car, an old Ford with isinglass (a kind of thin glass that shattered easily) curtains, and ran his fist right through the glass curtain, punching Bill in the nose. Bill stepped on the gas and got about a block down the road when his old Ford stalled. That's all Johnny needed. He ran down there, and the two of them got into a fight. It didn't last long, though. Bessie got out the other side and knocked Johnny out with a tire iron.

People did tend to settle their own differences in those days, the 1920s and 1930s.

Of all the great hunters of those days, the unquestioned ringleader was Farrell (Screwy) Lane. Dad and the Lane boys had a pretty good duck market going in Chicago. They would shoot ducks until they had enough to make a trip to Chicago worthwhile. Driving up there in those days was a long trip with bad roads.

Dad once hired Frank Rose to take a load of ducks to Chicago in a Model A Ford coupe. But they upset the car along the road, and the ducks spilled out. Nobody was hurt, so they put the car back on its wheels, loaded the ducks again, and continued on their way.

Not all of the trips turned out well. The game wardens were watching everything they did.

Dad and my brother Dallas once took a case of shells and went to Stewart Lake. The lake was frozen over, except for one air hole that was full of ducks. They chased the ducks out, hid, and then opened up on them when they came back. They killed about 250.

Meanwhile, the Lane boys had killed about the same number on another lake. But Farrell got drunk when they got into town. He wanted to talk to my dad but, of course, he was hunting. So he talked to my mother and set up a time for moving those hundreds of ducks to Chicago.

With all that booze in him, Farrell got careless. He was talking to my mother on a party line and someone overheard the whole scheme. The night they picked for the trip, the police were waiting for them. Farrell and his brother, Perry, had their own car. Dad had hired Frank Knox, who had just bought a new Chevrolet, to drive. I don't think the police realized that two cars would be involved. They knew the Lane car, which was leading the way. They moved in when Lane hit Fulton County, near Canton.

My dad, in the second car, realized it was the state police, so he told Knox to pull off on a side road. Knox refused, thinking they were being followed by a friend of his, Moody, who was a state policeman.

"It's Moody," he said, "he's OK."

That riled Dad a bit. "I don't give a damn," he said, "It's still the law and, we better turn off the highway."

Knox still wouldn't turn off, so Dad told him to slow down. When he did, Dad jumped out of the car and ran into a cornfield. Right after that, the police stopped both cars and searched them, claiming they were looking for stolen tires. They didn't find the tires, but they found the ducks. A lot of them.

The police arrested everybody and took them to Peoria, leaving Dad sitting in the cornfield, wondering how the hell he was going to get home.

He started walking. He walked for quite a while until a car pulled up alongside him and the driver said, "Get in, you lucky son of a bitch." It was Farrell Lane and his boys along with the state cop Moody.

The car was so crowded, Dad had to sit on Moody's lap, so the two were sort of chummy you might say. On the way back home, Moody said he had seen Dad jump out of the car but whispered to him, "keep your mouth shut and you'll get out of this."

Dad did get out of it, but he was the only one. Knox lost his new car, was fined $500 and given six months in jail.

Dad was smart enough to not keep doing things the same old way. The police were on to his "ducklegging" operation, so he found a new way to supply Chicago with ducks. He went to a Montgomery Ward store and bought a large cold-packing outfit and a canning machine.

We would buy No. 2 peach cans, kill a bunch of ducks, cold-pack them in those cans, then paste a peach label on the can.

We would buy No. 2 peach cans, kill a bunch of ducks, cold-pack them in those cans, then paste a peach label on the can.

After that, it was off to Chicago. Only, if we were stopped this time, we were selling peaches, not ducks. It was a hell of a lot easier because the cans weren't as bulky as the ducks. (By the way, if you want delicious ducks, cook them with peaches.)

Game wardens have been trying to catch the Hamms ever since I can remember. Dad had his problems with them when I was a kid and I had my problems with them when I grew up.

In the early 1930s, before Route 100 was put in by Bluff City, John Martin was the federal game warden out of Peoria. He used to spend good gas money driving those dirt roads, listening for the Hamm boys shooting at something down in Big Lake drainage, where we lived at the time.

Two of my brothers, J. C. and Virgil, were shooting ducks out of season when old John got after them. But they were young and fast and didn't have any trouble outrunning him. After they lost him, they hid their guns and went home.

John was like the old man who kept trying to shoot the rabbits that were eating his cabbage, but he couldn't hit them. He got on his knees and prayed, "Lord, if you don't keep those rabbits out of my cabbage, I'm going to kill every damned one of them." That's the way it was with John. He couldn't catch my brothers, so he went to my dad and told him if he didn't make the boys quit shooting ducks out of season, he'd have to arrest them.

Zeb Kost wasn't too bad of a guy, as wardens go. But he gave me a pretty good chase one day. I was shooting in a cornfield and came out at about dusk, when the law said we were supposed to stop shooting. I saw a car coming down the road so I hid. The car went by, then turned and came back, stopping on the road where I had been. It was Zeb. He sat there awhile and then drove off toward Bluff City. It was getting pretty dark by then, and I couldn't see whether he'd left or not. I came out of the field and started to walk toward home. Soon, I saw the outline of a car. Sure enough, it was Zeb. He'd turned around and come back and was sitting there, waiting for me.

I was climbing a fence to get back in the cornfield when he started his car. That made me hurry and I slipped, caught my leg on the barbed wire, and ripped a hell of a gash in it. I lay on the ground alongside the fence, hoping he might pass me. But damn his hide, he stopped even with where I was hiding.

Like a spooked rabbit, I jumped up and ran across the cornfield, putting ground behind me like a gut-shot deer. As I was running, I heard Zeb cross the fence, but I wasn't too worried because I was younger and had a good head start. He saw he was losing the race so he stopped, fired his gun twice in the air, and hollered, "Halt!"

That made me run twice as fast.

A few weeks later, I saw Zeb and showed him my leg. "Hell," he said, "I was just trying to scare you."

He sure as hell got the job done. I'm still carrying that scar.

Dad and I hunted furbearing animals all through the Sanganois Bottoms, by Crane Lake, Stewart Lake, and all the other small lakes and streams nearby. He knew those bottoms as well as he knew me. The water was deep and clear then, and the sloughs ran with a swift current. Those sloughs would be the last to freeze when subzero weather came. That's when we would walk along the shore, and the sky would be black with ducks flying to the open water. But as the weather got colder, even those sloughs would freeze. That's when the shame of the previous duck season would show up. It is something that still sickens me.

As we walked those sloughs and ditches, the ducks were there by the hundreds. But most of them were cripples. They would keep some holes in the ice open by swimming around in them. When they saw us coming, they would leave and hide in the flag patches and weeds along the bank. But not all of them could make it. Hundreds would try to escape, but their wings, feet, or tails were frozen in the ice. Many of them died from freezing or starvation.

I am partly to blame for that. So are my brothers and the other hunters because not one of us can say we caught every duck we ever wounded. Every duck we crippled, we tried to retrieve. I wish I could say the same for the rich hunters on the big duck clubs. To them, it was just a game. They couldn't care less about a wounded duck. Every duck shot by local hunters was put to good purpose. Either they were sold for food or money or were given away to someone who couldn't hunt but needed the meat.

My family has repeatedly suggested to state conservation officials that they should feed those crippled ducks. But they wouldn't do it. Hell, who would expect a Hamm to have any sympathy for the ducks?

I know one thing. The money the state uses for gas, airplanes, and unnecessary office jobs would go a long way toward saving some of those ducks.

F O U R

They called them the Roaring Twenties, but that didn't mean much to those of us who lived along the Illinois River at that time. We knew about Al Capone, and some of us even saw him from time to time when he came to the river to hunt. But his gangster life and Chicago were as far away from us as high-society life and New York.

But we did know Farrell Lane. He was one of us, and he pretty much ran things as far as market hunters were concerned. He had been a top booze runner for Capone and his gang out of Chicago. But when things got too hot, Capone came down to the Illinois River and hunted with Farrell.

Farrell had a casino and a beautiful houseboat that he always docked near it for important people who came in by train or car to shoot ducks. Farrell wasn't really a Capone type, not the way you've seen them in the movies. He didn't run around with a machine gun. To us, he was a fair man who happened to be boss because he had the connections in Chicago to sell our ducks. Also he was boss because he had money and we had none, and because he owned a beautiful

Farrell wasn't really a Capone type, not the way you've seen them in the movies. He didn't run around with a machine gun.

houseboat when all we had were jonboats. He was unquestionably the boss, and we accepted him as such.

I don't know how much money Farrell made. But he lit a few cigars with $20 bills, and he owned three or four automobiles at a time when the rest of us owned none.

Everything hinged on Farrell. That big houseboat was called *The Dinger*. It was big and carpeted and served as a bedroom for all of the big hunters from Chicago. Next to it was a building on stilts with a bar, poker tables, and crap tables. That was the casino. But it was nothing like the ones in Las Vegas or Atlantic City. All it was, really, was a bar on stilts where duck hunters went to drink and gamble. The casino was on an island about a mile and a half north of Browning.

I was just a kid then, but I usually would go with my dad when he took a group hunting. Almost always we would wind up back at the casino. Dad would go in and maybe play a little poker or drink a couple of beers.

Like all kids, I watched what was going on and wondered what it was all about. One day, I spotted some money on the floor. I didn't think I should touch it because I didn't know much about those gamblers, or what they might do if they caught me. But the temptation was too much. The temptation overcame my fear. I sauntered over and dropped something on the floor and came up with a $5 bill. I put it in my pocket and walked as quickly as I dared. A little later I saw Farrell and told him about it because he was the boss, and I sure as hell didn't want to get my dad or myself in trouble with him.

"Mr. Lane," I said. "I just picked up a $5 bill off the floor."

He looked at me across the room and scared the hell out of me until he smiled.

"Son," he said, "any money you see on the floor belongs to you. Don't ask no questions, just pick it up. It's yours."

You can count on it that I kept my eyes open after that. Anybody who dropped any money had to be pretty quick.

Unless he looked mean. Then I waited until I found out if he missed it or not.

After that, I had a lot of respect for Farrell. It wasn't until later that I learned that he ran booze for Capone. Things were tough in Chicago then. About one-half to three-quarters of Capone's runners got themselves killed over the money to be made during Prohibition. Farrell was lucky to get the hell out before a rival gang or the FBI did him in.

He was a different kind of guy. He used to keep a big bear chained up next to the steps that led to the casino. I never knew why he kept that bear there. He was just a tame old thing that didn't scare any of the local people. But later on I got a good idea why he kept it.

The FBI or some other federal agency raided the place. But they had to get past that bear first. It was on the steps leading to the casino. The agents decided they'd just look around outside instead.

That bear got loose once and destroyed most of a cache of whiskey that Capone's people had stashed back in the woods. We didn't see the bear anymore after that.

When I was a kid, my dad was a guide for Farrell. He would take Farrell's hunters out and get them a good shoot. Only some of them were Capone's people from Chicago. The rest of them came from all over the country. The one thing they had in common was money. And that was the most important thing to us.

Dad usually shot Yorkey Lake, but he also used Hawk Hole, Wiener Swale, Painter Flat, Chain Lake, and Eagle Point. I was usually with him, even though I was only ten or twelve years old. We got a lot of laughs out of some of those hunters. They would bring along yellow cloth to wrap around a stick, trying to make it look like an ear of corn. We had some better ways to show them. We always used some of our tame ducks for fly ducks and threw them out of the blind when a flight of wild ducks came over. The tame ducks just flew a few feet and landed with the decoys. Then the wild birds would just naturally come in.

One day, my dad and his group of hunters had their limit, so he took them back to the club. He told me I could stay in the blind and shoot while he was gone. I got drowsy and was about half asleep when some ducks lit in the decoys. I had a single-barrel shotgun and eased the barrel through the blind and pulled. I killed five or six and was as proud as I could be until I went to pick them up. That's when I found out some of the ducks were the tame ones we had tied to a trotline to use as decoys.

One of those flying decoys was a mallard drake I had raised. He was more of a pet than anything else. We kept him in a crate in the blind until a flight came over. Then we'd throw him out, and he would light in with the rest. Later, he would swim back to the blind, and we'd feed him.

Every night after shooting, we'd put that mallard and the other live decoys in a pen. But one morning, we went out to hunt, and they were all dead. Somebody slipped in during the night and killed them all. I felt pretty bad about that one in particular since he was a pet.

When hunters came back to Farrell's after a shoot, they would string their ducks to the side of the boat in bunches, just hanging there by their heads. That was a temptation for the boys from Browning. All of those ducks just hanging there like that, some of them could be turned into money or eaten by someone who didn't have anything else. But at the same time, they didn't want to get the wrong people riled up. So they went in there with a knife and cut out a duck here and there, leaving the heads in the cluster. I sure would have liked to have seen some of the faces when they took those ducks down and found just heads in the middle of the bunch.

Once, my cousin Jack and I got to snooping around in the woods and came across Farrell's big beer vat. It was sort of like a wooden horse trough. Farrell's beer was the clearest stuff you ever saw. It didn't have yeast in it like most of the other home brew of the time.

Jack and I found some reeds and used them as straws to suck the beer out of the vat. I liked that beer then and I still like it today.

F I V E

When I look out my living room window every morning, the first thing I see is the greenery of Grand Island about 200 yards away. Grand Island is one of the last remnants of life as it used to be along the major rivers of the United States. Grand Island is big—about 5,000 acres—with one big lake and one smaller lake. It runs for about 14 miles from Bath on the east bank of the Illinois River to Bluff City on the west bank.

It has always been a hunter's paradise and it still is, despite the fact that only a few rich duck club members who own it are permitted to use it. Legally, that is. The membership is mostly from Chicago and has been there for as long as I can remember. Some families have handed their memberships on down for several generations.

Grand Island is private all right, but I know it as well as I know the rest of the country on either side of it. I have wandered and hunted the length and breadth of it. During that time, I've seen the members and caretakers much more than they've seen me.

My family hunted it most heavily during the 1920s and 1930s, but we kept hunting it for a long time after that. We'd get on the island early, long before the members were awake. We'd get on the island in the afternoon when we knew they would have called it a day. We'd hunt there in season and out of season, it didn't make much difference to us.

Things haven't changed much on the island since we started. That's what makes it different from the rest of the land along the river. That also makes it valuable for those who own it. Now and then I hear people say the state should take Grand Island and open it to the public. I heard it one day while I was having a beer with a friend at Edo Long's Stag Bar in Havana.

"The state should just buy those people out and open it up," my friend said. "The members have got no more damned right to be there than I have. They just have a hell of a lot more money."

My buddy was no fool. I think he was just a little agitated because he'd just been caught trespassing there and fined. But his thinking was all wrong and I told him so.

"Look," I said, "if the state got Grand Island, there would be conservation officers patrolling it. They'd be staked out behind every tree, and no one would benefit from that. If they were there, it would spoil a playhouse you've been enjoying for a lot of years."

Last I heard, he was still going over there for a little recreation now and then.

Bluff City, where my family is from, is near the southern end of Grand Island. In the early days we were only about three miles from the best hunting you could imagine. The truth is, my family hunted Grand Island more than the club members did. It wasn't always ducks, either. We took coon, mink, and muskrat for a living.

We didn't use dogs when we hunted coons. I remember treeing many a coon and going right up the tree myself to shoot him or knock him out.

Our favorite place on the island was Bell Lake. We got to thinking of it as our own. Later, I hunted more on the Bath (or east) side of the river. That's when I got acquainted with Bill Drake, one of the Grand Island club members. We got to be friends. I saw him one day when he was on his way to do a little hunting.

"Dale," he said, "I'm going to your private spot on Bell Lake. I hope you don't mind."

I hesitated a second and shook my head slightly. "No, I really don't mind, Bill," I said, "but I sure wish you'd check with me first to see if it's OK."

We had a laugh out of that, but the two of us felt a kinship with Bell Lake. It's like a tenant farmer who's worked a piece of ground for years and knows it like he knows every tone of his wife's voice. Even though the place wasn't mine, it didn't stop me from feeling as if I was a part of it and it was a part of me.

I remember when my brother J. C. and I went to Ash Flat on the island during the last days of the season when the lake was frozen. We got there early in the morning, but hid when we heard someone coming.

Two men emerged from the brush and set up to hunt ducks at the very spot we wanted to be in. It was frustrating. They had shot after shot while we were hiding, waiting for them to leave so we could have our turn. After a while, when we were sure they had their limit, we both stepped out into the clear.

"Hey," I yelled, "you've killed enough ducks, damn it. It's our turn."

Things got kind of quiet. They looked at each other. Then one of them moved toward us. "Get the hell out of here," he yelled, "or you'll never get the hell out of any place again."

We got the message. I'm just glad our motor started so we could hightail it out of there.

Several years after that, Grover Holmes, who was the caretaker on Grand Island and one of the locals, told me a story.

"You know," he said, "some people have more balls than the National League. A few years ago, a couple of young punks tried to run one of our members and me clean off our own club."

He couldn't understand why that made me laugh. But he got to laughing, too, and we were like a couple of kids who shared a common secret.

My family used to go to the island to spear muskrats after the duck season ended. Holmes would chase us all over the lake, wasting a hell of a lot of time he could have spent hunting. After he got too old to run after us, he told me all he wanted to do was get close enough to visit. We didn't buy that.

Wrong? Hell, yes, it was wrong.

When we were hunting for the market, we went to the island in the middle of the night when it was below zero. The ducks would be sitting tight in water they kept open by flapping their wings. We'd move in over the snow with a sheet in front of us, then drop the sheet and start shooting.

Wrong? Hell, yes, it was wrong. I know that now, but I didn't know it then. It was just how we lived, how we kept body and soul together.

After shooting the ducks, we'd take them home and clean them all by hand. Not many people ever sit down and pick the feathers off two hundred ducks at a time, but I can tell you it's a long and boring job. When we finished, we'd haul those ducks to Chicago and sell them to the rich. So, in a way, they got their ducks back after all.

Once, Rodney Briney and three or four of us were on Grand Island, pot-shooting ducks over an air hole in the middle of the night. Of course, when we ran out to pick up the ducks, Rodney was green about the business. He broke through the ice, and he lost his shotgun. One of us went down there and got it for him.

We knew what we were doing, and we planned it every step of the way. Some people considered us notorious, but we never saw ourselves that way. It hit me one night when I had a conversation with Ed Hart, a member of Grand Island, in the bar at the Taylor House Hotel in Havana.

"Hell," he said to me after a while, "you seem all right to me. I kind of thought you people lived back in the woods somewhere like hermits and just came out once in a while to step from behind a tree and start shooting at people."

S I X

s far back as I can remember, we Hamms were the best hunters in the Illinois River valley. Over the years, we've taken thousands of people duck hunting—including judges, sheriffs, and Department of Conservation officials. Of all those people, I don't think there ever was one who didn't want to go again.

We know, of course, that efforts were being made on both the state and federal levels to stop our duck-hunting activities. But we never thought they would go so far as to use our habit of taking people hunting to set a trap for us.

Our family has always had a sort of built-in radar system to help us detect game wardens. But maybe we got overconfident this time.

It began one morning in the fall of 1956 when Bob Jones and I were down at the landing of my brother Dallas's resort. A car pulled in, and the driver introduced himself as Mark DeMarco. He said he was a louver salesman from East Peoria, and he asked about a place to hunt ducks. I told him I would take him hunting the following day.

The old radar was working fine, though, because as soon as he left, Bob looked at me and I looked at Bob, and we both decided we had better be careful around this man. We had a feeling he was a federal game warden.

The next morning, DeMarco was back and ready to go hunting. I took him to the Sangamon Bottoms, where we got into a blind for the day. It was legal to hunt ducks until sundown. When it came time to quit, though, DeMarco wanted to stay. I told him no, because I knew better than to take a chance.

While we were picking up our decoys, we heard someone shooting. I told him if I hadn't been with him I would have been accused of shooting late. That was the truth, too, because somehow the Hamms always got blamed for things other people did. We were used to it, but we didn't like it.

I took DeMarco hunting several times after that but never violated any laws. I never trusted him.

He was still around the next spring. I owned a tavern at Anderson Lake and was building a home across the road from the tavern. DeMarco would visit the tavern from time to time, and if I was there he would try to buy ducks from me. I would just tell him I didn't have any. Sometimes he would walk across the road while I was working on my house and try to sell me louvers and tell me what a good job I was doing. Then he'd try to buy some ducks.

He once asked to buy a hundred ducks for a brother who he said owned a restaurant in Chicago. I turned him down on that, too.

During 1956 and 1957, DeMarco and I spent a lot of time in duck blinds, swapping stories, relating our life histories, talking about women. He played with my kids and talked with my wife. He said what I wanted to hear. He gave me business cards and said I could call those people for references on him. He told me to ask some of the hunters in

Beardstown if he was all right. I finally gave in. And he played me for a sucker.

One evening, he walked into my tavern and said he needed a hundred ducks for that same brother with a restaurant in Chicago. I told him he would have to stay in the tavern, but I would try to get them for him. As always, I told him I didn't have the ducks, and that was true. But I knew where I could get them.

Once outside, I went over his car from one end to the other, looking for some evidence that he wasn't what he appeared to be. My radar was trying to tell me something, but I wasn't listening. His car seemed clean to me.

"I want $1.75 per duck," I told him, "and I want it in cash. And I want a receipt for a hundred tame ducks."

I went to see some family and a few other people and got his hundred ducks. I paid about $1.50 a duck. Then I went back to the tavern and put the wrapped ducks in his car. He was still standing at the bar where I left him. So I sat down next to him and told him where the ducks were.

"I want $1.75 per duck," I told him, "and I want it in cash. And I want a receipt for a hundred tame ducks."

"What the hell?" he said. "Don't you trust me?"

"No, by God, I don't," I answered.

Looking back on it now, I must have trusted him at least a little because I sold him the ducks.

By the time he left the tavern, he had paid me in cash and given me the receipt I wanted.

Before long, he called me for more ducks. I delivered him a couple of groups at two different times, adding up to about three hundred ducks and two snow geese. That was the last I saw of him until 1957.

That fall, he came back. He spent time with my brothers Pete, Dallas, and J. C. and his wife, Mary; Dallas's wife, Eva; and some cousins and friends of mine. He bought ducks from all of them.

I didn't know he was back. Had someone told me, I would have known for sure he was a warden. Some people just knew he was dealing with me, and that meant he was all right.

On September 5, 1958, federal and state wardens and a federal marshal met at three rendezvous points in three separate Midwestern states. They started before dawn. In Illinois, they gathered from Peoria to Beardstown along the Illinois River. They all had their watches set for 6:00 A.M.

That's when they knocked on my door. When I opened it and came out, they arrested me. And they had their guns ready. I told them my wife was gone, and I had to talk to my children before they took me away. They wouldn't let me go back in the house alone. So the officers and I went into the house as I talked to the children about what to do while I was gone. Then we left, and they put me in a police car.

After we got inside, I asked them what I had done. They told me I didn't have to worry, that I was not the only one involved. They didn't have to say any more because then I knew what it was all about. They took me to the justice of the peace at Beardstown.

When we got there, they had my brothers, sisters-in-law, cousins, and other friends. It was still early in the morning. They told us we needed to post bond if we wanted to stay out of jail.

I hadn't gone to the bathroom since I got up so I asked permission to visit the men's room. An officer accompanied me. He said his name was Townsend and was an assistant to the U.S. marshal. He asked me if I knew Bill Litell, the U.S. marshal out of Peoria. I said I sure as hell did, he was a friend of mine. Townsend went to the phone and called Bill. He asked him if he knew Dale Hamm. Litell said he sure as hell did. Townsend handed me the phone.

I spoke to Bill right then. He asked me when I was going to get him more fish and ducks. I said, "Hell, Bill, I'm not in a position to do that right now."

Townsend took the phone and talked to Bill again. He told

him about our problem, and that we all needed someone to post bond for us. Bill told him to let us post each others' bonds. Then Townsend and I went back upstairs. Townsend told the justice of the peace what Bill had said and the JP said that was all right by him.

It pays to know the right people.

S E V E N

I hired Lock Crissey of Lewiston as my attorney to represent me at the trial. Lock had me get two tame ducks before we went to court. I guess he was going to see if they could tell if ducks were tame or wild.

I pleaded not guilty because I had a receipt from the federal agent for tame ducks, but I was charged with selling wild ducks. I had a friend, Dr. Dan Morris, in Peoria at the tuberculosis sanitarium. Doctor Morris said there was no way the state or federal government could tell the bone structure of a tame duck from a wild duck. We also had proof that I had bought tame ducks from Earl Dixon. Russell Dixon and I killed those ducks. We hung them up and shot them. We hauled them to Chicago and sold them for wild ducks. Those Chicago city people didn't know the difference.

I could prove that I raised tame ducks at my home at Anderson Lake. Nobody saw where I got the ducks I sold to the agent except my friends and relatives. I did not have any ducks of my own at that time. If I got on a stack of Bibles, I couldn't tell you whether those ducks I sold the agent were tame or wild. But knowing where they came from, I could guess pretty close, and so could anyone who knows the Hamms. But it was up to the prosecutor to prove his case.

My trial was held in federal court in Peoria. Judge Mercer presided.

Lock put Mark DeMarco on the stand as his first witness. Lock asked him how many ducks he bought from me. DeMarco said he bought 100 ducks in January 1956 and another 100 a few months later and 120 later on, which I delivered to his home in Pekin.

Lock asked him what he did with all those ducks. DeMarco said he stored them in a locker freezer in Springfield. Lock asked DeMarco if he had the only key to the locker. DeMarco replied that he did not have the only key, there were other keys.

"How do you know then that these were the same ducks that Hamm sold you?" Lock asked him.

DeMarco said he couldn't be sure. By that time, Lock had him in a pretty good sweat. I could see the beads on DeMarco's forehead.

Next on the stand was Lawrence Merrill. Lawrence was my neighbor. He also worked for the state. The U.S. attorney asked him how long he'd known me. He said all of his life. He told them he watched me grow up, and that I worked for him, taking care of Chicago duck hunters during the season.

They asked him if I'd ever raised tame ducks. He said I didn't. He lied through his damn teeth. He knew I had tame ducks because in the fall they would fly to his house. But he lied because he knew he might lose his state job if he didn't side with the state.

The next witness was a state biologist. He was going to show the jury the difference between tame ducks and wild ducks. He brought out five shoeboxes. Each shoebox held a dead duck. Some of the ducks were larger than others. He told the jury that the smaller ducks were pintails and you can't domesticate pintails.

I told Lock to ask the biologist if pintails and mallards ever mated. He did and the biologist said they did, occasionally. To me, that took care of his testimony regarding telling if a duck was tame by its size. A cross between a tame and wild duck will be smaller than a wild duck.

The judge called me to the stand next. I had a choice. I could testify or invoke the Fifth Amendment to avoid incriminating myself. I asked Lock what to do. He said I should take the stand. I told him I couldn't testify that the ducks were wild. He said I should say only some of them were wild. I took the stand.

The prosecutor asked me about that. I said what Lock told me to. I was so damned scared I didn't know what to say. But after I thought it over, I wondered why the hell I said that. How could the jury find me not guilty when I just admitted I'd sold wild ducks?

After that, Lock told me to change my plea to guilty and get it over with.

Jim Curless and Vince Connor, the state game wardens, predicted I'd get six months in jail. Judge Mercer gave me three years' probation and a $1,550 fine. I paid the court costs, only $50 in 1959, but didn't have the $1,550.

After the trial was over, I ran into both Lawrence and Lock again.

I was madder than hell at both of them. I told Lock he wasted the taxpayers' money to go to trial and then have me blow the case on the stand like that.

I never did pay him.

I met Lock awhile after the trial at a tavern. He asked me about his fee. I told the bastard he had a lot of guts to ask for a fee after he sold me down the river with that stupid advice.

Over the years, by the way, Judge Mercer has eaten a lot of Hamm ducks. He was a fine judge.

I met Lock awhile after the trial at a tavern. He asked me about his fee. I told the bastard he had a lot of guts to ask for a fee after he sold me down the river with that stupid advice.

E I G H T

The story in the Pekin Times said three men had been arrested at the scene of a wrecked car on August 17, 1963. The three men were myself and my dad, Pete, and my son Ronald. The story was a damn lie.

Here's what happened.

The Department of Conservation had held its annual duck blind drawing at Browning that day. After it was over, some of the boys decided to go to Bluff City at the levee and kill some wood ducks, even though it wasn't duck season. I heard about it, so Gene Richardson and I decided to go over there and watch.

When we got there, we found my son Ron and two game wardens, John Schoonover and Tom Logsden. I got out of my car and walked over to where the wardens and my son were. I asked what the problem was, and John said my son had been shooting wood ducks. I said, "Where are the ducks?" John said there weren't any ducks.

I told John even the federal boys don't make an arrest unless they have some evidence. John said he was going to give Ron a ticket for something. So I said to John, "Give him a ticket and let's get out of here."

John decided to give him a ticket for having an uncased rifle, which was in the trunk of Ron's car. I said go ahead, but there shouldn't be any tickets issued for shooting wood ducks out of season. John agreed to that.

He made out the ticket, and when he gave it to Ron I looked at it, and he had made it out for an uncased rifle and attempting to shoot wood ducks.

With all the legal trouble our family was having, I had planned to send Ron to law school. I knew having a record would be a problem. So I asked John to let me see his ticket book. He gave me the book, and I took the ticket and told John that wasn't what he agreed to do. I had a mind to tear up the ticket, but I didn't.

While we were still standing there, three cars pulled up. It was the boys who had been at the Browning drawing. There were about fifteen of them, and they were feeling no pain. They began to harass the two game wardens. Then they started throwing bricks at the wardens' car.

Tom and John got into their car and locked the doors. I thought sure as hell the boys were going to push the car into the river with the wardens still inside. I told them they were headed for trouble if they didn't stop. They stopped, but then they lay down behind the car so the wardens couldn't leave. My friend Gene Richardson joined them. I told Gene, who had a government job, he'd better get the hell out of there before he ended up getting fired.

While the boys were lying on the ground, someone went around the side of the wardens' car and let the air out of the tires. Then they finally got up.

I thought they'd set nails under the tires, so I went up to the windows and told Tom and John not to move. So they sat in their cars until everyone left. That's when they discovered the air was out of their tires. All they could do was walk to Anderson Lake, about three miles, for help.

Gene, Pete, and Earl Hamlin and myself were up the road,

talking about what had happened when Pete mentioned the air being out of the tires. So we decided to go down to the car and help them out.

When we got there, the car was still there but Tom and John were gone. By this time, it was getting dark. The wardens saw us coming down the road as they were walking out. They were scared, and hid in a cornfield until we left. Then they started walking to Anderson Lake again.

Pete, Gene, Earl, and I headed for my tavern at Anderson Lake. By the time we got there, the boys from the Browning drawing had left. Somebody said they'd gone to Beardstown. That wasn't quite right. Where they went was back to the wardens' car, where they proceeded to take a wide board and ram it through all of the glass that car had. Then they beat the hell out of the car until it was demolished. Then they went to Beardstown. And so did we.

When we got there, we found the boys at the Melody Lane Tavern. They were having one hell of a time. It looked like one of those taverns out of the Wild West. They just took it over. There was a band in there that night. When the band took a break, they left the bandstand. Bad decision. The boys got up on the stage and tried to play the instruments. When the musicians returned from their break, they were upset. That's when all hell broke loose.

My son Ron was right in the middle of it. Gene Richardson and I were at the bar, just watching. I told Ron to come over to the bar, which he did. All three of us stood there, watching. I told Gene he was going to see one hell of a show now, which he did. The boys tore up that place—tables, chairs, bandstand, and the rest

When the police came in, they broke it up and ordered everyone out. I started to walk out with a bottle of beer in my hand. An officer said I'd better put it down or they'd take me in. The outcome was one of the musicians had his leg broken, and the rest of them got the hell beat out of them.

I know the boys got fined pretty heavily. And the Melody Lane Tavern never reopened. They finally just tore the building down.

Meanwhile, the wardens got to the tavern at Anderson Lake. They were convinced that I'd helped wreck their car. They filed charges against me and eighteen other guys.

The sheriff and the states attorney contacted me and said, "Dale, if you will plead guilty to those charges, we'll drop the eighteen other warrants. We'll drop the charges against them, and they'll help you pay your fine."

I went ahead and took the rap. I didn't have a lawyer, I just took the rap and got those guys all off. Only one of those guys came forward to help pay the fine, and that was Earl Hamlin. He gave me $50, but I paid about a $400 fine.

I'd forgotten I was still on probation from that Mark DeMarco deal, or I'd never have agreed to that. This was two years later, and I'd gotten three years' probation. I had a job with the state, repairing highways in Fulton County. An assistant U.S. marshal and a deputy came out to the job we were working. That deputy was so big he could whip a bear with a switch.

They came up to me and showed me their credentials. Right there on the job in front of everybody, they put a belt around my waist and handcuffed me to the belt. They took me to jail in Springfield because I'd violated my probation by pleading guilty to that job.

The most embarrassing thing I'd ever had happen to me in my life was them coming up there and looking for Dale Hamm. Here I am, got a nice state job, and that really makes it tough. That's room for them to fire me. I think the only reason they didn't fire me was they knew I didn't tear up that car.

They kept me in jail in Springfield for a week. Then an assistant marshal from Peoria came down. The U.S. marshal up there was still that friend of mine. I knew him before he ever became a marshal. His assistant came to get me. The people at the jail in Springfield said, "Well, aren't you gonna handcuff him?"

"No, we don't need to handcuff him," he said. He just took me out to the car. He loaned me a dime for the telephone so I could call my family and tell them I was going to Peoria.

This marshal was supposed to have me handcuffed and in the back seat. But I rode in the front seat. He knew I was getting a raw deal, but he had his job to do and he did it. They locked me up in Peoria, and I had to get a lawyer to help me get out. So that's what I did.

I spent about a week in jail in Peoria. I still owed the government $1,550 from my fine when I was arrested in that duck-selling incident. They forced me to pay that before they let me go. I borrowed the money and paid it. Luckily, my lawyer was a friend of mine and he didn't charge me.

After I got out, my wife picked me up at the jail, and we headed home. But we stopped at a tavern in Banner first. I wasn't ready to go home, so I told her to go on home and I'd catch a ride. I stayed until the tavern closed.

When I left, I hitchhiked to Little America and called my boss on my old job with the state highway department. I told him to pick me up at Little America so I could go to work. He did, and I went back on the job that morning. I didn't want to lose my job over something that wasn't right.

After I got out, my wife picked me up at the jail, and we headed home. But we stopped at a tavern in Banner first. I wasn't ready to go home, so I told her to go on home and I'd catch a ride. I stayed until the tavern closed.

N I N E

Back in the early days, the Sangamon Bottoms was the Home of the Mallard. More ducks used to come down that flyway than any other in the country. Before they changed the channel, the old river was open for public hunting. We called that part of the river "the firing line."

The boys who lived in that area who had no place else to shoot came to the firing line. The Sherrill boys, the Robison boys, Jeep Bolinger, and the Winstons, all local fellas, used the firing line. My brother Dallas, Oris Lamb, and myself used to go out there the night before to get a spot. But we always had company. The boys from Browning would hold the blinds for the pay hunters out of the big cities. That was one of the ways they had of making a few dollars.

This type of hunting lasted until the Depression hit in the early 1930s. But that's when the hunting got better for those people who were really hunters at heart.

Knapp Island and many other private clubs folded during the Depression. That gave us access not only to the firing line but to what used to be private clubs. My dad and us boys used to go up around the old Rainbow Duck Club after the members had given it up. We would go into the swamp and scare up ducks by the thousands. All we had to do was find an opening in the timber and wait for them to come back. We didn't have to have any decoys, just duck calls. After we would kill a few, we would push a stick into the mud somewhere in the opening and hang one of our dead ones on the stick. It looked just like a real duck sitting out there. The ducks would see that and, with a little toot on the duck call, they would come right to us.

We didn't need a blind, we just stood behind a tree. The main thing in shooting ducks is to be sure you don't move when they are around. Ducks have much better eyes than we do, and they are also up high where they can see you much better.

The good hunting lasted for several seasons, and that's all my father and us boys did. But my dad knew this couldn't be the only thing for us to do, since now we were old enough to go to work.

When I was a kid, I was a water boy, hauling water to the farmers in the area. I shocked wheat for them in the fall. The first real job I had was at a hemp factory, that must have been in 1933–34. In 1936 I went to Peoria to work at Baker-Hubbell Dairy, I peddled milk. See, I haven't been a river rat quite all my life. I left there after eleven months and went back on the river and hunted a while.

My two sisters, Glenna and Wanda, got jobs at Sutliff and Case Drug Store in Peoria. Jobs were hard to get in the 1930s, but Dad used to take the Sutliff and Case people duck hunting. In return, the store manager gave my sisters jobs.

They worked there until about 1939. They rented a house down on Sixth Street. That winter of 1939 was colder than hell. Our dad loaded our furniture into a farmer's stock truck and all of us boys, except Dallas, got into the back of the truck and left our happy hunting ground for Peoria.

We had been hunting furbearing animals. When we got to

Jobs were hard to get in the 1930s, but Dad used to take the Sutliff and Case people duck hunting. In return, the store manager gave my sisters jobs.

Peoria, we sold the fur to buy a load of coal for that house on Sixth Street. This was probably the toughest period of our lives. All we knew was how to hunt and fish. But Dad came through again. He knew a man by the name of James Bainter who worked for R. G. Letourneau Equipment Company on North Adams Street. Of course, we used to take Jim hunting with us. I remember the first time I took him, we got to the blind, and I discovered I hadn't brought my gun. I settled the problem by doing the calling and Jim did the shooting.

He told my dad to send me to Letourneau and put in my application for a job. But, due to a lack of education, I didn't pass the entry test. That hurt me very deeply, but I didn't give up. I took it a second time, then a third time. I guess they got tired of seeing me, because they gave me a job anyway. Of course, I am sure it was Jim's doing. It sure wasn't my schooling.

The Letourneau plant was located on the Illinois River. It had turned cold and the lake across from the plant had frozen. I could see ducks sitting in an open hole in the ice. I asked Ward Cruse, an employee at the plant, if he wanted to try and kill some of the ducks that night after it got dark. He said he would like to try. I borrowed a pair of white coveralls from a friend of mine, Bruce Barnes.

That night, Ward and I started across the ice. There was snow in some places and it was clear in other places, which made it look like open water. We had learned years ago never to go out on the ice at night unless we took a long pole. I was holding one end of the pole and Ward had the other end. I would cross the clear ice, and I could feel Ward pull back on the pole and circle that clear ice as much as possible. When we got fairly close to the ducks, we could hear them calling. We laid on the ice and crawled on our stomachs toward the sound of the ducks. With those white clothes on and the cold weather, the ducks never paid any attention to us.

When we got close enough to shoot, I told Ward, "Let's let

I got married in 1940. I bought a lot on Caterpillar Trail on Route 116 in Peoria and built a basement house on the lot.

them have it." We emptied our guns, then we shot the ones we had only wounded. After that, we took the pole and dragged the dead ducks out of the water hole. By that time, my partner had gotten a little braver.

We had cord in our pocket and tied all of the ducks onto the cord. I guess we had about fifty of them. We realized this was very poor sportsmanship, but if a guy didn't have his own club and wanted a few ducks to eat, that was one of the ways to get them.

I worked about three months at Letourneau and became a labor foreman. Eventually, almost all of my brothers went to work there. Dallas came to Peoria later and got a job, too. We did all right, for river rats.

Our mom and dad bought a big house at 509 Ravine Street, and we all lived there. The kids paid them rent. We were doing much better than we ever did down on the river. But we couldn't forget that way of life. One by one, we eventually migrated back to our old stomping grounds—the Sangamon River valley. A million dollars couldn't buy what we'd learned there from our father.

Dad was the first to go back. The rest of us were all married and had families to take care of. I got married in 1940. I bought a lot on Caterpillar Trail on Route 116 in Peoria and built a basement house on the lot. My wife, Bernice, and I lived there until 1945. Then I was drafted into the service.

The day before I left Letourneau, though, I beat up one of the bosses. I had been a foreman but had gotten mad and quit that job and went to the welding shop in the same factory. I stayed there two weeks, and they put me on production, and I was making good money. The union had gotten in by then

After a few months, they told me I was up for welding inspector. But I didn't think I had enough experience yet so I passed. After another three months, they came back and said "You're up for inspector again." This time, I took it. I was doing good and had a nice, white shirt on and wasn't getting dirty or anything. That was a hell of a good job.

Then I wanted to go hunting pheasants in South Dakota. My boss gave me permission to go. But when I came back, I found out my boss hadn't told the superintendent he'd given me permission. The superintendent suspended me with no pay for two weeks. We got right into it then, see. I didn't tell him I had permission to go, because it was duck season any- way, and I just went duck hunting for two weeks. But when I came back, I started raising hell over it.

They wanted to fire me. One of the bosses there kept watching me to see if I made any mistakes so they could fire me. One day, I passed six parts without inspecting them. Old man Letourneau needed them in a hurry, so instead of me taking a print and checking the parts, I just passed them on without inspecting them. They were put together backwards. That gave them the chance to fire me, so they did.

I filed a grievance with the union. We had a big meeting, and I pleaded my case. I told them about the pheasant hunt- ing, and that I had permission from my boss but he didn't tell anybody. The company said we owe Hamm his job back and some back pay. So I got my job back.

That's about when I got called into the service. The night before I was to report for duty, I stayed up until about eleven o'clock. I'm still mad at this guy for snitching on me about the backward parts. I went over to Letourneau's and stood behind his car, waiting for him to come out. Pretty soon, here he came. I was watching through the back glass to see which side of the car he'd get in on. When he walked up to open the door, I stepped out and said, "You dirty son of a bitch." He took off running toward the plant, and I was cracking him and knocking him down. A friend of mine, Russ Dixon, came by and jumped out of his car and said, "Dale, quit it and get out of here because the cops are going to get you."

I let the guy go. The next morning at seven, I got on the train for Chicago to report to the military. About nine or ten

When he walked up to open the door, I stepped out and said, "You dirty son of a bitch."

o'clock, the sheriff and a deputy came to my house, had a warrant for assault and battery on this guy.

"If you want him," my wife said, "you have to go to Fort Sheridan to get him. He's already gone." Of course, I had that planned.

We had two children at the time, Ron and Caroline. A third was on the way. I spent about a month in the service. They sent me to Germany. I was trying for a dependency discharge. When my company officer heard my story, he wondered why the hell they drafted me in the first place. He said that if what I had told him about having a family was true, I would be leaving very soon. He checked the story and in a few weeks I was on my way home.

After my discharge, I started to build a new home on top of the basement one we lived in. Through friends, especially my brother-in-law Woody Carter, we managed to get it built. I didn't have cash enough to complete it, so I borrowed from the Tazewell Savings and Loan Company to finish it. That was the first decent home we ever had.

But I was never satisfied. We loved the river valley, and that's where I wanted to live. Every weekend when we were off work, I would come to the river and hunt ducks. For the fun of it, I would always bring a friend or two with me.

We went back into the Sangamon swamps and killed all the ducks we could carry out. The guys I brought with me to hunt usually couldn't hit a bull in the ass with a paddle, so I'd kill all the ducks.

A bunch of us—my brother Dallas, Jack Binns, Kenny Dew, Forrest Tittsworth and myself—went hunting one day in the Sangamon Bottoms. It was Armistice Day. It had turned cold and the wind blew like a hurricane. We got lost for a while. When Dallas found his boat, it was sunk. We managed to get back to a grain elevator in Bluff City. A man named Fred Florin let us come in his house, get warm, and dry out.

"If you want him," my wife said, "you have to go to Fort Sheridan to get him. He's already gone." Of course, I had that planned.

Jack, Kenny, Forrest, and I got in a boat and took off. It was so windy we could hardly move. The motor conked out, so we had to start rowing. If we kept moving, we were all right, but that's where Forrest failed. By the time we got to Farrell Lane's house on stilts, Forrest was almost finished. We had to help him out of the boat and into Farrell's house. We gave him some of Farrell's dry clothes and thawed him out. I think he missed a few days' work over that ordeal.

T E N

In about 1947, I had an opportunity to buy a small farm at Anderson Lake. A part of it extended into the lake. It was ideal for me because I liked the hunting and fishing I could call my own. But I didn't have the money to buy the property.

I talked to my father. He and Fred Shearer had leased land at West Point in the upper end of Anderson Lake. My dad taught Fred all the fundamentals of duck hunting. Now, he approached Fred about buying the land. The man who owned it lived in Macomb. My dad and Fred drove over there and bought it. A few months later, I got a down payment for the property, so I went to Fred, and he gave me a contract for deed on the property in exchange for the down payment.

A couple of years later, I sold my house in Peoria and moved to a house in Bluff City with my mom and dad until I could build on the farmland at Anderson Lake. I built a double garage and breezeway for a living room. We used that double garage for living quarters. We lived that way until about 1956. By then, our children were growing and we needed more room. I decided to build a house and attach it to the breezeway.

One spring, far from duck-hunting season, a friend of

I built a double garage and breezeway for a living room. We used that double garage for living quarters.

mine named Merrill Emmons and I decided we would go duck hunting at Anderson Lake. On the way, we met another friend, Dean Farwell. He told us the federal wardens had been going to the same end of the lake we wanted to hunt.

In those days, Merrill and I didn't much care. We decided to go hunting anyway. Since it was spring, the roads were muddy. We thought the feds wouldn't go in because of the mud. Merrill had a Jeep, so we went ahead.

The ducks were plentiful at the upper end of the lake. Merrill parked his Jeep along the road to the lake and we waded out into the water. We had a hell of a good hunt. We had about thirty mallards—all drakes except one hen. One of us shot that by mistake. We finally ran out of shells and decided to leave. As we were leaving, we could hear my brother J. C. and my cousin Gary Hamm shooting ducks. They were down the lake a ways from us.

As we approached the Jeep, I noticed a coat lying in the weeds along the road. About that time, a federal man jumped from under the coat.

I told Merrill we'd better take a different way out because the federals might be waiting for us. We walked about a mile out of our way, hid our ducks, guns, and coats under a brush pile along the road we came in on. Then we walked to the Jeep. I told Merrill if anyone was there, let me do the talking. As we approached the Jeep, I noticed a coat lying in the weeds along the road. About that time, a federal man jumped from under the coat. After he showed us his credentials, I told him we were trying to catch the people who were shooting in the lake, and he was just the man we needed to help us catch the hunters. I told him I was raising crops for the state (which was true), and if I didn't keep hunters out of the area, I'd lose my contract. Since he was new to the area, he believed the story—to a certain extent.

He told us that there were two other agents with him. We stood and talked awhile. I was wet and started to get chilly from not having a coat. I told the agent I was cold, and he lent me his coat. Then he asked us to walk with him down to where the other agents were. We got to the Jeep, and he told us to wait there.

While he was on his way to get the other agents, we could still hear J. C. and Gary shooting. They had come in by boat, but the agents didn't know that. They thought we were all together.

Soon, all three agents came back. The other two I happened to know, their names were Harms and Blasovitch. When Harms saw me he said, "Hamm, what did you do with the ducks you shot?"

"Harms," I said, "just because my name is Hamm, I had to be shooting ducks. Do you think we are the only duck hunters in the country?"

About that time, the boys in the lake shot again.

"Listen to them shoot," I said. "I'm glad I'm standing here, otherwise I'd get the blame for that."

I told him about the state contract I'd lose if I didn't keep hunters out of there when the season wasn't on. Harms decided to give up. But Blasovitch didn't.

"You might as well shut up," Harms told him. "He'll just lie to you anyway."

Harms asked us to take them along the lake in the Jeep. It was beginning to get late in the evening. When we reached the area where the boys were shooting, Harms told Merrill to turn the Jeep toward the lake. He did. Then Harms told him to flash his headlights. He did that, too. Just then the boys shot about six times. One of the feds said, "Listen to them. They're raking [bunch shooting] them now."

Merrill flashing those lights was just a warning to J. C. and Gary, so they took off in their boat. As we were leaving, Merrill got the Jeep off in a ditch on purpose so it would look like we were stuck. That would give the boys some extra time to get away.

When we finally got to the highway where the feds had left their car, they separated Merrill and me. They began to question us. I told the agent it was getting late and I had to work in my tavern. About that time, I heard a noise in the other car. I thought they might be giving Merrill a bad time.

"They won't get rough with Merrill will they?" I asked the agent.

"No," he said, "they don't operate that way."

I told the agent I had to be getting home. I got out of the Jeep and started walking down the road. Harms rolled down his window and told me to come back. I did. He took my license number, and then they let us go. Merrill and I went to the tavern.

J. C. was in the tavern when we got there. We got into the beer pretty good. At about midnight, we decided we'd go get our guns and ducks. J. C. came with us.

First we went to Merrill's farm. We thought we'd play it smart and get a horse to ride to get the ducks. J. C. and I mounted up, but the horse was smarter than we were. When we got on, the horse sat down. We got off, he stood up, and we got on again. This time, he went down and damn near broke J. C.'s leg. That was enough of that.

We drove out there in the Jeep instead. We parked it and walked the rest of the way and got our ducks and guns.

E L E V E N

’ll tell you what happened to me one time. I was at Bluff City, and a guy, a stranger, came up to me and wanted to go duck hunting. He had a canoe. I took him down the river and I went out. This is when I was young, just a boy. He got me out there, and as it turned out, he was a federal warden. He was trying to catch me doing something.

He said, "We'll put the decoys out here, but don't lean over in this canoe."

So we got out there and put out decoys. Pretty soon there was one out there where I wanted to grab it, and I leaned over to get him, and the warden dove right out into the river because he knew that canoe was going to roll over. I'm still sitting in the canoe. I didn't get a bit wet. He swam to shore and I paddled. To this day, I don't know what ever happened to that guy. I got him a good dousing, anyway.

During a duck season in the 1950s, J. C. Hamm, Farrell Lane, Bob Hamm, Pete Hamm, and myself decided to go poaching on Central Gun Club.

During a duck season in the 1950s, J. C. Hamm, Farrell Lane, Bob Hamm, Pete Hamm, and myself decided to go poaching on Central Gun Club. It was late in the season. We crossed the river at the pump house in Big Lake Drainage, walked across the riverbank to the lake.

Market Hunters

There was a boat parked along the lake, but no one was around so we decided to use it to get to Upper Point, which was part of Central Gun Club. Thinking the owner of the boat was not going to be there that day, we got on Upper Point, got in Central's blinds, and began shooting ducks. We were having a hell of a good time. Until we heard someone coming.

We kept quiet as the boat approached. Pretty soon we heard someone holler for J. C. We thought it was one of our boys yelling, but that was our mistake. It was John C. Herring and his son-in-law Bob Burgett. Herring happened to be the owner of the boat we had borrowed.

He was hotter than hell at us, but he didn't know who we were. The first thing he did was order us off the property. We got into a hell of an argument, and pretty soon Herring and Burgett were cocking their guns.

It finally quieted down, and we went to the boat. We took it back where we found it, with Herring following us all the way. As we walked back to our boat, he fired his gun in the air. Burgett was walking next to me and told me not to argue with Herring, he was just too mad.

We got back in our own boat and went across the river to the pump house. Herring was still following us and still madder than hell. We got in our trucks to leave, but Herring went up to the pump house, where Bob Hoppings, the attendant, was and knocked on the door. Hoppings's wife, Barb, answered the door. Herring asked her who we were. While he was asking her, Burgett was standing behind him shaking his head for Barb not to tell. Lucky for us, she didn't.

At least that time it was duck season. Pete, Bob, and myself hunted Central plenty of times when it wasn't. One of those times I remember, the lake was frozen solid enough for us to walk on the ice. We had a sled with us in case we killed any ducks. It's easier to carry a bunch of dead ducks on a sled than it is to carry them.

We thought it was one of our boys yelling, but that was our mistake. It was John C. Herring and his son-in-law Bob Burgett. Herring happened to be the owner of the boat we had borrowed.

We crossed the lake and saw the ducks sitting along a levee in open water. When a group of ducks are on the lake, they'll keep a spot open, no matter how cold it gets. Usually it's a pretty small hole, so ducks are packed in wing to wing.

Pete, Bob, and I got behind the levee and snuck up on the ducks. We raised up when we were close enough and shot into them. We killed about fifty. We got all the cripples picked up and put them on the sled with the dead ones. That's when Pete looked up and said, "Hell, Dale, there comes someone down the levee from Central clubhouse."

We grabbed our guns and took off across the lake, pulling the sled loaded with ducks. The caretaker for Central back then was Andy Taylor. But we didn't know whether it was Andy coming down the levee or a game warden.

We were going like hell across the lake toward an island in the middle. Whoever that guy was, he was gaining on us. I told the boys to get the ducks into the timber on the island, then I got behind a tree and waited. When the man got within a couple hundred yards of me, I fired my gun in his general direction. I am sure the shot hit the ice near him because he turned, and all I could see was his ass going the other way.

About fifteen years later, I decided to open a tavern on Bath Chute. That's when I got to know Andy Taylor pretty well. He was in for a beer one day, not too many people around, and Andy and I got to reminiscing on the old days.

Andy told me that once, about fifteen years ago, he was shot at by one of the Gobel boys from Browning. I began to grin. Then I began to laugh.

"What are you laughing about?" Andy asked me.

"Andy," I said, "I know it isn't funny but that wasn't the Gobel boys doing the shooting, it was me."

He thought it was funny. I guess in fifteen years the statute of limitations for scaring the hell out of somebody is up.

T W E L V E

I never saw Edo Long smile my whole life. But, inside, he was smiling all the time.

Roger Wickman was smiling most of the time, but he was a Jekyll and Hyde. He might smile at you one minute and hit you in the snoot the next. Roger was full of shit, but he wasn't a bad person. He was always willing to give you a hand at least.

Edo and Roger built themselves a duck blind. Edo had owned a duck club, but he sold it to Willis Cole. So he built this blind, and the three of us decided to take the blind to Central Gun Club. By this time I was respectable enough to lease some land to hunt on Central—legally.

Edo's blind was built on telephone poles. We took a jon-boat and pushed the blind downriver, about twelve miles to Central. We parked the blind inside a spillway, which belongs to Central. A few weeks later, along about September, Roger and I decided to get the blind and put it in a suitable spot for hunting. Before we left in my boat, I suggested to Roger we should take our shotguns and try to kill a squirrel in the pecan trees on the riverbank. So we took our guns and got in.

By the time we got to Central, we switched to a boat we

had down there. We had some squirrels by then, so we put them in the boat with us. While we were taking the blind to our spot, I cleaned the squirrels. We got the blind set up and headed home.

I didn't have my gun in a case, which is illegal. Roger didn't have a hunting license. I told him before we started back upriver what to do if we met a game warden. I'd head the boat into the bank, grab the guns, and run as fast as I could into the woods. Sure as hell, we just came around the first bend and there were two game wardens in their boat.

The wardens signaled for us to stop. That was my cue to go.

The wardens signaled for us to stop. That was my cue to go. As we passed them, I shouted over to them that we'd be right back. Instead, I opened up the throttle and ran up into a ditch, hit the bank, and told Roger to take care of the squirrels and I would take care of the guns. Roger took care of the squirrels all right, he threw them out onto the bank. If he'd just tossed them into the water, they would have sunk.

When the wardens pulled up, one of them stayed with Roger, and the other proceeded to try and catch me. I was running like hell through the brush.

The warden came to a clearing, and when he looked to the left, I was running to the right. I looked back and saw which direction he was looking and ran into the brush so he couldn't see me. I kept running for about a mile until I reached my friend Allen Sarff's, house. I asked Allen to take me to Bath to the Brick Tavern.

I went into the Brick and sat at the bar to have a beer. I was still a little excited, and this old, nosy barmaid name of Mary asked me what was my problem. I told her it was none of her damn business. As always, she couldn't take a joke. You had to know Mary to appreciate her.

I proceeded to tell her what happened. I said I expected Roger to show up pretty soon. About then, I looked out the window and saw Roger coming in. And who was with him but that no-good warden.

They came into the tavern, and Roger told Mary he needed $100. That's when Edo Long walked in. Roger told Edo he needed $100. Edo pulled it out of his pocket and gave it to Roger on the spot.

In the meantime, the warden walked over to where I was sitting and said, "What did you run for?"

"What the hell you talking about?" I replied, "I've been sitting here, drinking beer."

Roger and the warden left and went back to their boats. One warden told the other warden I was up at the Brick, drinking beer

They gave Roger three tickets. One for four squirrels taken without a license, one for operating a boat without the proper marking on the side, and one for not having enough life preservers. They knew Roger wasn't operating the boat because we passed them while I was at the motor. But there wasn't much he could do about it.

We didn't think the wardens had a good case, so we contacted my son who is an attorney. We took it before a judge. The wardens took an oath on the Bible to tell the truth. I don't think they did.

They got Roger on all three counts.

I should have my ass kicked for not getting up in court and telling the truth. But the wardens didn't tell the truth, either.

I couldn't hunt raccoons, either, without getting into some kind of trouble.

Some boys I knew from Chicago wanted to go coon hunting with me. Our dog treed a coon up a cottonwood tree. Of course, cottonwood trees, you have to be very careful because their limbs will snap easy. They're not like a maple tree or some other sturdier trees.

Our dog had that coon treed, and I could climb to the moon, that's how good a climber I was in those days. I climbed up there to that coon, and he was right at the tiptop. I was afraid to get too high because one of the limbs would break. So I'm shaking him. You know how the waves are in the ocean? My shaking worked the same way and made the damn coon seasick. Oh, he got sick, and he'd been eating grapes. He had a bowel movement, and I want to tell you what, it came down and got in my eyes, my nose, he just covered me. I thought I was going to fall out of the tree.

I could watch him up there, so I knew I had him loose, except his two front feet. Everything else was just shaking. I never did get that coon out of the tree. But he damn near got me out.

T H I R T E E N

All the hunting and running through the woods we did when I was younger got me in pretty good shape.

I took about twelve guys hunting up in the Sanganois years ago. They followed me through the sloughs over to Crane Lake. We shot ducks up there. The night before, we had an argument about one of those guys. He had played football in college and was now the sheriff over at Fox Lake. We got on him about not being in good enough shape to keep up with us.

After we started out of Crane Lake, I took off through the woods, just trying myself to see how fast I could go and give them a fit. I had them strung out about a block long or longer. That big football player, the first thing he did was start throwing his ducks away to lighten the load. The other guys would pick them up. And then he took his boots off and started walking in his socks because he had blisters on his heels. He's coming down through there, trying to keep up.

When I'd take a notion to rest, I'd sit down. But about the time they'd catch up to me and be ready to sit, I'd jump up and take off. They had to keep walking and never got to rest.

Myself and another fella got to the boat, and just for orneriness we started along up the slough to pick them up. They were all worn out, lying on the bank. Instead of going and getting them, we pulled in below them a ways and said, "If you guys are going with us, you better come on down here." We wouldn't go pick them up.

We got them in the boat and came in to my tavern at Anderson Lake. The big football player sat down there and took his socks off. The backs of his heels, an inch wide, were rubbed raw. When he went back to work, he had to cut the heels out of his slippers and wear them to work until he healed up.

Some years later, I went to Sand Slough down at the foot of Crane Lake and heard these guys hunting out there. They were a bunch of guys I knew from Browning, and they were trespassing on Crane Lake. Well, I wanted to hunt where they were, so I sneaked up on them. They heard me coming and got scared, and I ran them plumb out of there.

I'm not proud of some of the things I've done and the way I hunted. A young man will sometimes do things he wouldn't do when he gets older. With age comes wisdom.

I went ahead and shot ducks there. The next time I saw those Browning guys, I told them who it was who ran them out. They said that was a hell of a note, that I ran them out and they'd walked three miles to get there.

When I tell these stories about the things we did, don't take it as boasting. I'm not proud of some of the things I've done and the way I hunted. A young man will sometimes do things he wouldn't do when he gets older. With age comes wisdom.

Too bad I wasn't a little wiser one day when I took a group of hunters to Grand Island. One of them was one of my sons, Ron, who was about twelve at the time. He had the time of his life that day, but we damn sure broke the law.

The other hunters with us that day were Harry Wedge, Jim Hamm and his sons, Bob Hamm, and Bob Jones. We went to a place we called Ash Point Flat on Grand Island, when the weather turned cold and in came some rough snowing and blowing. The ducks started coming back from the cornfields, right into where we were waiting.

We started shooting them on the wing, and we weren't hitting much. When it started to get dark, the ducks came in to us by the thousands. We'd fire a box or two of shells every round. They were landing in front of us at very close range. It was after dark and we could hear them. We couldn't see them, but we could hear them come in and light.

I said, "We're going to wait until we get three or four bunches to light. Then I'll tell you when to raise up and shoot."

We would all wait and shoot together. It was so dark, you couldn't see. We'd all rise up and fire at once, then go out into the water and see how many we could find. You can't imagine how many ducks we would kill with each volley.

My brother J. C. and Stanley Briney were shooting at the other end of the lake. They told us later, when we got back to the tavern, that they'd never seen anything like it. They said it looked like the Fourth of July when our muzzle flashes lit up the dusk.

A lot of people will say, "Well, that's a hell of a sportsman." I understand that. We were young and we did it. Back then, we thought it was funny. As I look back, I can see that it wasn't funny at all.

F O U R T E E N

We got away with more than we got caught with. My brother J. C. and I went over on Grand Island at about nine or ten o'clock at night. It was pitch black, no lights on our boat. We're not used to having lights on our boat. People know where we're at if we do.

To this day, I don't know how many we killed that night. We ran into the middle of them with that motor wide open. They jumped up to fly when we ran into them, and that's when we shot them.

The next day in the tavern, I told everybody, "Boys, I'm going to tell you right now you can run up on those ducks at night with an outboard motor and knock the hell out of them."

But the interesting part about anything you do in the sports world is talking about it, getting in the bar and having a little conversation about it. Hell, it wouldn't be any fun if you had to keep everything a secret.

Like when Earl Shawgo, Al Chapin, and I went up on the Sangamon one time on Ash Swale, which is a refuge for the ducks now. We were standing up there shooting these ducks. Of course, it was state ground then, too. But our neighbors had a little patch down there, and they didn't like it because we were going on their land and shooting ducks. So they kind of got the game wardens on us.

The wardens came into the club, and we were shooting up there, and they told the wardens what to do and how to do it. The fact is that one of the guys who owned this little club was a state game warden. The wardens came in and walked up to catch us.

"When you see the ducks jump up down the way," I told the guys, "you'll know there's somebody coming."

Sure enough, the ducks jumped up and I said, "Boys, they're comin'."

So we just moved across the slough. They came up there and before they got to where we were, they had to cross the slough, too. But it was deeper where they had to cross. So they had to go back to where they started, get across the slough, and come up the side we were on.

Instead of me leaving, like I should have, I didn't do it. We stayed and killed probably two ducks over the limit. By now, the wardens were coming up the same side we were on. They came up and got within twenty yards. They never saw me. One got up there and said, "How you doin' Dale?" Walked right up behind us. They started talking to us and found the one or two extra ducks.

They'd walked a long ways to get to us. I said, "Boys, why don't we go back the way we came out instead of your way?" I carried the ducks out. I didn't have to, since they'd taken them from us, but I carried them out anyway. I treated them real nice. We put them in my boat and went back.

We got our tickets and had to go to Beardstown. When we were on our way to Beardstown, the wardens ran a damn stoplight, and the state police picked them up. The state troopers that stopped them, they knew us. Now the way I see it, the wardens were in worse violation than we were because they were endangering people's lives by running the red light where we were just duck hunting. Anyhow, the wardens only got a warning ticket.

When we got to Beardstown, the justice of the peace fined us $105 apiece. When we got done, we went over to the tavern. The wardens went with us, and we all sat there and enjoyed ourselves and had some drinks.

Another time, J. C., Bob Lashbrook, and I went out on Swan Lake in the middle of the night, and the snow geese were thick in there. We shot into those things, and they got up and started coming around out of there like crazy. J. C. reached right up and grabbed one right by the leg. We were putting them in a gunny sack, and he stuck that one right in the gunny sack with the rest.

We didn't have any time, we had to get out of there. We didn't know who was going to come up on us.

Merrill Emmons and Jim Haubensauk and Frank (Peanuts) Bolton and I went up in a boat on Anderson Lake. They didn't like Fritz Shear, who ran the clubhouse. I think the state had taken it over by then. He's a guy my dad and I both hunted with. He did me wrong, too.

These guys go into the Anderson Lake clubhouse and start pouring fuel on the damn floor. Me and Merrill got the hell out of there. They set it on fire, and Peanuts damn near got caught in there.

I got the blame for it. You hear stories about that today, they all say I did that. I wish I'd written down all the stories people have come to me and said they heard about me. It's always some other guy told them something about me. I just grin and let a lot of them think it was true.

That's like Don Crandall, who used to go around and tell a story about us. You know, when we couldn't find anyone else to fight, the Hamms would fight among themselves. But Don said we got into it one night and tore up a whole tavern, demolished the tavern. He exaggerated that, but if we get a few drinks in us and take a notion to battle each other, we'll

You know, when we couldn't find anyone else to fight, the Hamms would fight among themselves. But Don said we got into it one night and tore up a whole tavern, demolished the tavern.

do it. Then we shake hands the next day. As far as us tearing up a tavern, that never happened but he'll tell that story yet today.

My reputation sometimes got me arrested when I didn't deserve it. I remember Don Hamman, who owns Central Gun Club, asked Kenny Seilshott to take some of Don's friends out to hunt. They had been goose hunting in southern Illinois so they came through here. Well, Kenny wasn't going to be there. He went goose hunting or some damn place.

So Kenny called me and asked if I'd take them out to the upper end of Crane Lake. It was Don's land and Kenny was renting it out. So I took the guys out there to the blind and got them all set up. I stood outside the blind because there wasn't enough room in the blind for me. I stood out there, had my gun with me. They knocked down a couple of ducks. I went out to get this cripple. When I got out there, I didn't have any idea that the warden was around, but he wasn't thirty feet from me at the most.

I got the duck and hit his head over my gun barrel and hung him up in a tree. I hollered to those guys in the blind to tell them where it was, then I took off. I was going pretty good. I don't know why, but I was. I went on through there. Then one of the wardens came after me. I walked to my truck, and Edo Long and Roger Wickman were there. I was talking to them and looked up and saw the warden come out.

"Were you hunting down there?" he asked me.

"No, I wasn't," I said.

He and I had a conversation, and he didn't attempt to arrest me or anything. But he had those guys in the blind arrested for shooting over a baited area. Kenny had it filled full of corn. It was plumb full of corn.

After the warden gave them tickets for all that, he called Kenny. Kenny denied everything. He said he wasn't there and didn't have anything to do with it. So when the wardens got done giving out tickets, I got a letter in the mail saying I was

aiding and abetting. They were hunting over a baited area, and
I helped them get in there, see. So I get a damn ticket. I did-
n't know they'd baited the damn thing. I hadn't hardly ever
been down there. That was the first day I'd been there.

I felt like I was innocent, and my son Ronnie thought I was
innocent.

["I defended him in the case," Ron says, "He pleaded not
guilty," and we went to trial in Springfield in front of the U.S.
magistrate. The testimony came out that he was there, he
hadn't fired a shot, he just brought these guys down. In fact,
he left his boat for them and walked back. He didn't know
either of the guys who were hunting.

"The judge still found him guilty. I didn't put Dad on the
stand. Later, the prosecutor asked me why I didn't put him
on the stand. I said I didn't feel it was necessary, all the evidence we wanted came out in the government's case. The
prosecutor said, 'I had every article that's ever been published
about your dad saying what a poacher he was. I was going to
put that into evidence, and I probably would have got him six
months in jail if he'd have testified.'

"Rather than that, Dad was fined about $250 and that was
it."]

F I F T E E N

Once I moved back to Bath after leaving Peoria, I have never left again.

I was in the tavern business at Anderson Lake, had a farm with a couple hundred hogs, built grain bins, and worked at the power plant in Havana. But I always went back to hunting. Nineteen fifty-six was one of the better years of duck hunting. There were more ducks then than we'd seen for years. After that, though, the ducks started disappearing. And the Hamms didn't kill them all, either. It was farming practices, droughts, predators, drying up the habitat—those things cut down the population.

Market hunting pretty much dried up after my arrest in 1956. I didn't have much time for it with my other work. Market hunting didn't pay. The market's always been there, but when you don't need to do it, why take the risk? It still exists today. When some of the boys get a chance to sell some ducks they'll sell them. There'll always be somebody who wants ten or twenty ducks for a party or something. The Chicago market, though, has ended.

For me, going duck hunting was like going to work. We were going off to make money. But then there was more money to be made in the tavern business.

There'll always be somebody who wants ten or twenty ducks for a party or something. The Chicago market, though, has ended.

When the water came up, it floated. I proceeded to build a tavern on the old, wooden hull. I ran that for a good many years.

In 1966, I was getting divorced from Bernice and decided to start over again. Pot Clark, a commercial fisherman, had a block of land adjoining Bath Chute. I left my resort at Anderson Lake and bought that land from Pot. He had an old, wooden barge. It was sunk and had a lot of ice in the end of it that spring. I got a fella to help me and we chopped the ice out of the hull and patched the holes in it. When the water came up, it floated. I proceeded to build a tavern on the old, wooden hull. I ran that for a good many years.

Finally, a guy came along, and he was a little bit ornery anyway and he had a little money. He'd come in the tavern and kind of take over. The ceiling was low, and they'd punch it with their fists when they got to drinking. I had to stop them from that. One day I said, "If you guys want to do that, you just better buy the place." So this guy said, "How much you want for it?" I told him. He gave me $500 right there for a down payment.

I had remarried by then. I went home to the trailer and told my second wife, Betty, I sold the tavern. The guy who bought it ran it one year and folded up. He and his wife got a divorce over it and everything. I bought it back again. It was on the bank back then, and it was in bad shape. I went over there with a match and burned it up. It was impossible to fix.

A guy told me that there was a barge in Chicago by Brandon Locks, the last lock before you go into Lake Michigan. I went up there and bought it. I got a trailer and a pickup truck, so I took my boat and trailer up there. I loaded the truck and trailer on the barge and got ready to push it down the river with a 40-horse Mercury motor and an 18-foot jonboat.

"Where are you going with that barge?" the old guy I bought it from said as we got ready to go.

"Havana, Illinois," we said.

"Well," he said, "I'll never see you guys again."

He didn't think we knew what we were doing, and we

were going to get in a hell of a lot of trouble. I got it out there in the canal and we were on our way. After a few miles, they had a slip that they'd pull in to let other barges pass. When I got there, the guy backed out. He was closing the canal.

Five people from an office came out to see what was going on. One of the women looked at us and said, "It looks like it'd have been easier for you to drive that truck downstate instead of hauling it on that barge."

"Well, it would have been, lady," I said, "but the barge wouldn't fit on the pickup."

It was early spring and there were snowflakes falling. My deckhand, Fred Miller, and I stayed on the river all day. We came to one of the locks downriver. The lockmaster knew we were coming and helped us in and helped us out with no trouble. But at the next lock, we had plenty of trouble. First, we tied the barge to a tugboat. It got tied up the wrong way by some deckhands there, and the current swung the barge around and rammed it into a concrete wall. I thought it was going to crush my boat. But it just had enough room that it skinned my motor up a bit and went clear.

We got through that one, but then we were tied off in the lock. That water drops forty feet. We tied off when it was high, but we tied off in such a way that the rope would slide as the water went down. Except my buddy tied it so it would-n't slip. When we started down, my end was going fine, but his end was holding.

"Release it!" the lockmaster screamed at him. But he couldn't, and I'd already warned him to keep his fingers out of there or he'd get them cut off. The lockmaster ran and got a fire ax and cut the rope. Then it came on down with the water.

Five days after we left Chicago, we arrived in Bath. We tied up the barge by my house and built a new tavern on it. It's been there ever since.

The floating tavern got to be pretty famous when a

reporter for the *Los Angeles Times* wrote about it for his paper.

I'd run excursions. People would come from Springfield by the busload, and we'd go around Grand Island. I had a license for that. I had the barge fixed so they could sit on top, take their food with them, and party. Then we'd take a black-jack table, and a gal to run that, and a crap table and poker table and had the first little casino on the river. That was illegal, of course, but that's what we did.

Until 1985, when I sold the floating tavern, I worked there, or was around there, all the time, especially on the weekends. I went down there on the weekends and helped tie up boats to the tavern. Had to help out those girls in bikinis, you see.

S I X T E E N

E verybody would always ask me, "Where do you hunt?"

"I've got everything from Havana to Beardstown," I said.

Which is the truth. If we took a notion to hunt on Grand Island, we did. If we took a notion to hunt on Central, we did. If we had a notion to hunt on Crane Lake, we did. We hunted on all these areas all our lives when we wanted to.

But we didn't abuse them because we knew these people personally, and most of them were friends of ours. I've never been arrested for trespassing in my life.

The way I did it, I poached on the Sanganois and all of them, but I made it a point not to let them catch me. Because when they catch me once, they'll say, "Now, Dale, I'm warning you. Don't come back anymore." So I don't have to get that first warning if they don't catch me the first time.

You get out early, you pick the time when they come in. A lot of times they'll come in at noon, and you go out in the afternoon. Or you know they won't be there in the morning, so you get out there early and get ducks before they get out there. They could hear our motor sometimes, so we'd park on one side and walk across. When the first shot was fired, we'd start looking over shoulders.

I owned my own duck club on Quiver Creek, which is up by Goofy Ridge. I bought it for $10,000 and turned right around and sold it for $20,000. It was the perfect club—four acres of ground and only one duck blind. That was in the 1950s or early 1960s. Eddie Hickman and I killed more ducks up there than anybody ever dreamed of killing. Most of the time, I had to find more private places to hunt.

They caught me on Grand Island one time shooting teal—me and Mike Korth and Eddie Hickman. It was on Bell Lake. The caretakers came up and snuck around to get to us. When they got there, I said, "Where are you boys going"? They said, "We were just checking to see who was shooting in here."

"Well, I suppose we'd better go," I said, "would you go out and pick up those teal for us? I don't have any boots on."

They went out and picked up our teal, then they walked over to our boat with us. I said, "Now boys, if you want us to get out of here, you'll have to help us pull this boat back into the water because it's a hard thing to get back in the water." So they helped us put the boat back in. They had to run us out, of course, that was their job. But they never had us arrested.

But there were plenty of other times I hunted legally and helped push on the clubs around here. When I came to live in Bath, I started hunting with Edo Long. He had the Lakewood Supper Club and the Lakewood Duck Club just north of here. I'd go up in the morning and eat breakfast with them and then help take care of the hunters for him.

We had a guy by the name of Ernie Layton who hunted with us. He was a guide up there. He'd get them in the blind, then whenever the ducks would come in and his hunters would get up and shoot, he'd ask them "What'd you shoot for?" He was serious about that. He wanted to kill all the ducks.

One time he came down there in his car, had his gun in the car, pulled it off, and shot a hole right through the top of his car.

Edo and Roger Wickman and myself and Jim Smith used
to go to Edo's club in the spring and have a spring shoot occasionally. We never did get caught up there. They finally did get
wise to Edo and had him arrested a couple of times. I think
half of it is who you know on this stuff.

After I hunted with him a couple three years, I went to
Central Gun Club and ran that a good many years. The funny
thing about it is I eventually got invited in the front door of a
lot of these clubs I used to poach on, Central and Grand
Island included.

What happened was, the original Central Gun Club folded up. Jack Canterbury and another fella bought it and invited me to hunt with them. Then they sold it and Don
Hamman bought it. I leased it from him for seven or eight
years, the whole works. It was about 2,000 acres. Then I'd
lease out duck blinds to whoever wanted one. I'd find a spot
and put a stake up and that's where they built their blinds.

In about 1982, I was kind of crowded out of Central. The
duck clubs around me were jealous because we were having
good luck. They tried to lease it out from under me. I was
paying $8,000 a year for the lease, and they offered $15,000.

Every damn one of them got woke up in the middle of the
night because one night I got about half crocked, and I sat
down at the telephone and called every one of those sons of
bitches up and told them what I thought of them. Some of
them wrote me letters, and some apologized, and some
never responded at all.

They were going to have a meeting about the lease. The
owner, Hamman, had a partner named Don Heil. They were
going to meet at Central Gun Club. They didn't tell me anything about it. But a good friend of mine said, "Dale, they're
pulling a dirty trick behind your back. They're going to lease
Central out from under you for $15,000." I said, "That's nice,
I'm glad they told me."

So Don Hamman came down to my floating tavern. Don

*After I hunted with
him a couple three
years, I went to
Central Gun Club
and ran that a good
many years. The funny
thing about it is I
eventually got invited
in the front door of a
lot of these clubs I
used to poach on,
Central and Grand
Island included.*

and I and Kenny Fletcher and Joe Joseph were on the back porch of the tavern, talking. The other guys knew what was going on, so Fletcher and Joseph, when the subject came up, they got the hell out of there because they knew the shit was going to hit the fan. Fletcher stayed until I said to Hamman, "What about this meeting you're going to have?" He said, "I don't know about any meeting." I said, "You're a lying son of a bitch."

Of course when I said that, we jumped up, Fletcher got out of the way and the fight started right there on the porch. We fought from there, into the tavern, and ended at the other end of the tavern. I had a nephew sitting there, and he was going to help me. I said, "I don't need any help, you stay out of it."

Hamman said, "I don't want any trouble." I let him up, and he went out the door and back to Chicago.

Then, I went to the meeting at Central. They were all in there and I walked in. I said to Jim Martin, "There you are, you big son of a bitch, you're the one who started all this."

I had a check for $1,500 in my pocket. So it just happened that I got there in time. Ed Heil spoke up and said, "You guys take this part and lease the other part to Dale." One of the other guys said they'd lease it to me for $4,000. Hamman and Heil wanted the money, so I pulled out the check and handed it to them.

They were supposed to pump water to us and take care of it, and all I had to do was take care of my hunters. Well, come the season, they didn't pump any water to me for fifteen days of the duck season. So I just refused to pay them the other $2,500 I owed them.

They hounded me for that, but I told them they'd done me wrong, and now they got a little of their own medicine. That was the last year I ever had anything to do with Central. At least, officially.

S E V E N T E E N

Now that I'm eighty years old, I've mellowed some-what. All the hunting clubs around here like Grand Island and Crane Lake, all of them, we've had our dif-ferences. But in my later years, I've been invited to hunt on all of them. The thing I enjoyed about that was that it was just pleasurable. A good time. I didn't have to worry about any-one shooting at me or chasing me away.

It turned out to be like that with a lot of people. I guess I just lived long enough to let bygones be bygones. Hell, I for-got more things I've done than I can remember. Maybe they did too. Like Oscar Lynn. He's the one I threw in the water in my younger days. We eventually became good friends. I leased duck-hunting ground from him. We got along good—after we'd had our run-ins.

I ended up trying to help a lot of these clubs I used to poach on, instead of hinder them. Some of the clubs ask me for advice on where to build their levees or where to plant their feed for ducks. I try and help them the best I can.

I realize some people will think that what we used to do was unfair to the game and to the landowners. When I was growing up, we followed in our dad's footsteps. My father

All the hunting clubs around here like Grand Island and Crane Lake, all of them, we've had our differences. But in my later years, I've been invited to hunt on all of them.

raised eight children back in the 1920s and 1930s, and things were very hard. Hunting and fishing became our way of making a living.

In our later years, my dad and I and Paul Davidsmeier, who runs a hunting club near Snicarte, organized the Duck and Goose Hunters Association. In the 1970s, we realized that our duck population was depleted. We felt like we should try and replace some of the ducks we'd killed. Now, partly through our efforts, we have seen quite an increase in the population of ducks in our area. It's my way of giving something back and making up for the ducks I took illegally.

I'm doing it for the younger generation's benefit. My grandchildren and great-grandchildren are coming up now. They hunt, but not like we used to. We're trying to show them a different way of life other than hunting and fishing for a living. They're all getting their schooling, and that's the way it should be.

As for me, when I look back, I wouldn't change what I did for any office job. I just wasn't ever cut out for it.

Now, partly through our efforts, we have seen quite an increase in the population of ducks in our area. It's my way of giving something back and making up for the ducks I took illegally.

LORE, LEGENDS, *and* LIES
EPILOGUE

LORE, LEGEND*S*,
AND LIE*S*

One thing Dad always liked to do was get ahead of people when they were walking through the woods, then hide and scare the hell out of them when they caught up.

Back in the late 1950s, his brother J. C. told him, "Dale, you've got to come down here and look around the pond. I found some tracks and I think they're bear tracks."

J. C. took him along the pond just below our house, and sure enough, there were bear tracks there. Dad got a bunch of guys together, and they had a big bear hunt. They spent a day and a half looking for this bear. It was fifteen or twenty guys. They all had guns and were out hunting this bear. Then, J. C. couldn't stand it any longer. He had to admit that he made the bear tracks himself.

You talk about hot. He bought that whole story. The sinker was clear past his Adam's apple and he was hot.

I was at the Anderson Lake tavern one day when John Dutton came running in and said, "There's a lion down in the field by Bluff City." The crew got together. I mean, this crew could get together in about eight seconds. They were going to attack this lion. They get down there and there's a big collie dog lying there. It was Merrill Emmons's dog.

—*Ron Hamm*

I was helping Dale dig a well. Benny Seckman and I were down about thirty feet at the bottom.

About that time, Dale's cousin from Peoria came along and asked him to go have a beer with him. So they got in the car and left for Havana. With Dale gone, we had no way up out of the hole.

We started hollering for help, and Kenny Dixon came over and winched us up out of the hole. That was a funny feeling to be down that far with nobody on top.

Another time, we were digging a septic tank for a school-house. When we got there in the morning, we saw a snake in the bottom of the hole we were digging. We had an argument over who was going to use the revolver. Dale grabbed it and shot that snake.

Must have been seven or eight feet down. He shot it right through the head. Never saw anything like it.

—Leo Curless

I was seventeen or eighteen years old. I believe it was Christmas Eve, and Dad wanted me to go coon hunting with him because his dog wouldn't tree a coon. I didn't want to go. It was snowing and cold. But, we went.

We got out there, and his dog takes off into the woods. But my dog, Tammy, wouldn't leave me. She wouldn't help out at all. She'd go off a little ways and then come right back to me.

Dad had given me this lantern to carry. I was swinging it around and hit my anklebone. When I hit it, I grabbed Dad's arm and was yelling, "Ow! Ow!"

About that time, Tammy came running out of the woods, and she was mad. She thought he was hurting me. Dad's yelling at me, "Get her away from me!" I got ahold of her and pulled her away, but she was ready to do battle.

—*Sue (Hamm) Tarvin*

The first I remember of him, I was too scared to meet him.

When I was a kid, my dad would push for hunters on Grand Island. He parked behind Dale's house by a ferry. Dale kept chasing the young kids away from the water, afraid they'd get drowned or whatever.

I'd sneak down there and try to get in my dad's truck. I'd hide from him down there in the morning. He ran me back up over the hill with a belt, chasing me.

That's the first time I started to get to know him. Ever since then it's been quite a pleasure. Most of the time, in the baseball off-season, is when I hunted with him. It's like a cartoon going out there hunting with him.

We get in this boat down there, and you have to pump the bulb on the gas line to keep the motor running just to get out there.

The one thing is, when he tells you to get down because there's ducks coming, that's when you want to get up because that's when he starts shooting.

You hear stories, but you really don't know him from the stories. It's an adventure every time we go out there.

I can't think of any better time I've had hunting than I've had with him.

—*Mark Clark*

When I was in the eighth grade, I got a gun for Christmas. It was a .410 shotgun. Hunting was our whole life. When I was little, I remember Dad always being in his hunting clothes like he was on a safari or something.

I grew up learning to run a trotline and how to bottle fish and hunt squirrels. I went with Ronnie to trap mink. Dad wouldn't take me duck hunting because of the cold. I would have complained too much.

—*Marilyn (Hamm) Ford*

I have been duck hunting since I was eight years old. Now, in my forties, a particular hunt he took me on is the best of my life.

Dale was leasing blinds at Central Gun Club in 1983, and whenever possible he would try to take Dad and me along. He picked us up about 12:15 P.M. that day, and we headed for Central. It was a weekday, so Dale thought there wouldn't be too many hunters.

When we arrived, there were only a couple of vehicles at the clubhouse. We loaded our gear in the boat and headed for the lake. Entering the lake, we met Jim Swinford and his dad, who were coming in with their limit of mallards. They said the ducks were flying pretty good and to go ahead and use their blind.

It was a clear, cold, windy day. We loaded our guns at 1:15 P.M. Jim Swinford was right, there were ducks in the air everywhere. They were coming out of Crane Lake and going into the cornfields. Dale was on my left and Dad on my right. Just to be there with those two was enjoyable in itself. Both were in their late sixties, and both had seen more ducks than I'll see if I live to be a hundred. But to watch them in the duck blind, you would think it was their first hunt because of how excited they were.

Both are excellent duck callers and shooters. Dad was on the duck call as we watched the sky. We hadn't been in the blind five minutes when the first bunch of mallards started working. A bunch of twenty-five to thirty swung into the wind, working to the call. With the bright sun shining on them, we could tell they were mostly drakes. They were about ten feet over the water when we took them. When we had emptied our guns, five drakes were on the water, four dead and one crippled.

Dale hollered for me to get in the boat with him to go after the wounded duck. He ran the motor and put me up front to shoot the duck. If you're a young hunter like I was, you soon know who's in charge. We started across the lake with the 25-horse motor wide open. There were small whitecaps on the lake, which made it a rough ride.

Dale was standing up, yelling at me to get ready to shoot. I was having enough trouble trying to keep upright on my knees, let alone shoot the gun.

Dale saw the duck between waves with its head low to the water. "Shoot the goddam thing!" he yelled.

I came up on one knee, trying to balance myself with the other leg and put the gun to my shoulder. Just before I pulled the trigger, the duck dove under the water.

"Damn it," Dale yelled, "you're going to lose him!"

He banked the boat to one side, throwing me on my side while I was trying to keep my gun upright.

"Get up and get ready to shoot the duck," he yelled again.

Back on my knees with the gun to my shoulders, I waited for the duck to surface. About fifteen seconds later, which felt like an hour, his head surfaced. Just as I fired the gun, a wave hit the side of the boat, and I missed the duck by a foot.

"Oh, no!" Dale yelled, "you missed him! Goddam it, you missed him!"

By this time, the pressure was on, and I knew I'd better hit the duck or face the wrath of Dale's blood-curdling yell again. Luck was with me the second time, and I killed the duck.

We picked up the other ducks and headed for the blind full throttle. When we got there, Dad was calling and there were ducks all over. Within five minutes, a bunch of around 150 mallards worked to the call and came into the decoys. At the end of an hour and fifteen minutes, we had 19 mallards to take in—15 drakes and 4 hens.

If we'd stayed, I don't know how many ducks we could

have killed. But Dale said we'd had a good hunt, and it was time to quit.

When we reached Bath, I took a picture of Dad and Dale with the ducks. When I look at that picture, I still remember the thrilling one hour and fifteen minutes of that November day at Central. I don't think I'll ever have a more memorable hunt.

—*John E. Fletcher*

Back in about 1960, I saw him about as mad as I've ever seen him. He went hunting one day, poaching on Crane Lake, and he went into one of the duck blinds up there. He got himself all situated in the blind. Then he looks down at the willow on the front of the blind, and there was a name carved right in the willow, "Dale Hamm."

He hadn't even been in the blind, and the last thing he needed was publicity that he'd been poaching in someone else's blind. He just raised hell about that. He took his pocket knife and cut his name out. He found out later that Bob Perry had been in the duck blind and carved Dad's name in it.

—*Ron Hamm*

We were going to shoot some geese a little out of season. We got in Dale's car, and he didn't have a license plate on it.

Of course, a policeman stopped us right away. Dale had two guns loaded in the car, and I didn't even know it. He told me to let him do the talking.

He got out to the policeman, ran like hell right up to him. Dale was almost crying. He said, "Me and this other old fella here, we don't have any money, and we were gonna hunt rabbits for dinner."

The policeman let us go, must have felt sorry for us, but told Dale he'd better get some license plates on his car.

As soon as this guy left, we went right out and shot some geese.

—*Harold (Itze) Ellsworth*

We went to a place Dad was renting called Horseshoe. It was just a piece of ground the Spoon River ran through. He had it for a couple of years.

This day, it was Dad, me, Eddie Hickman, a couple of friends, and my brother-in-law. It was the first time my brother-in-law had ever gone hunting. This was during teal season. We'd been baiting the area and went down there to hunt teal.

We were standing in timber along the water, and there weren't many teal, but there were wood ducks, which were out of season. But we proceeded to kill wood ducks. We probably killed forty or fifty, then we'd take them in the trees and hide them. My brother-in-law, this being the first time he'd hunted ducks, didn't have a waterfowl stamp. I didn't have a plug in my gun, either.

We'd been there an hour and a half or so, and we're having a good shoot. We could see better than a quarter of a mile down the water. I looked down the bank and, way down there at the end, comes a guy through the water in chest waders.

"Who's that guy?" I asked Dad.

Real calmly, he said to me, "If that's who I think it is, we won't be hunting anymore today."

We stood there for the fifteen minutes it took him to get there. If I'd known it was a warden, I could have put a plug in my gun and told my brother-in-law to throw his gun in the river. But, I didn't have any idea. I thought Dad would have said something.

The guy comes up and says, "I'm a federal warden and I'd like to check you out." I about had a stroke.

We showed him our licenses. He started running shells up

into my gun until he couldn't run any more. He said, "What's the deal with no plug?"

Then, he unzips the pouch on his waders and pulls out a Glad bag. It was full of feed he'd picked up out there. "Well, boys," he says, "I'm going to have to arrest you for hunting over a baited area."

About that time, two more federal wardens came out from behind us. Our dog was running all around, and we were scared he was going to start dragging those wood ducks out from where we hid them.

My brother-in-law got ticketed for no stamp. I got ticketed for no plug. And we all got ticketed for hunting over a baited field.

We were walking out of the timber with the wardens, and that dog kept jumping up and grabbing Eddie's coat. Eddie stuck his hand in there and found he had a wood duck in his pocket. He stuck it back in and the wardens didn't see it.

We got back to our trucks, and after the wardens left, we wondered whether we should go down there and get those ducks. Dad and I went to Havana and had a couple of beers, then we went back, and he ran down and got the ducks. It cost us $135 apiece.

Another time, down there at the same place, we were baiting again, and we walked down there to hunt. We had a blind built down there that year. When we got there, there were two guys in our blind. Dad was pretty even-tempered, for a change.

"What are you guys doing?" he asked them.

"We're hunting ducks," they said.

"You got permission?"

They said, "Yeah, we do. We got permission from Dale Hamm."

"Dale Hamm, huh? OK," Dad said, "we were just checking."

Then he walked behind a tree and got a gunnysack full of

corn we kept there. He went out in front of the blind and threw that corn out just as hard as he could.

"What are you doing?" those guys asked him.

"I'm just trying to help you boys kill a few ducks," he said.

We left and went back in the timber about a hundred yards and stood where we could see those guys. Pretty soon, they took off. They must have got nervous about hunting over bait. Of course, they had been anyway, but they didn't know it.

—*Don Hamm*

Dale and I and another friend of ours, Jim Gibbs from Clinton, went out hunting. Anyplace Dale wanted to go in and shoot, he had what I called "a floating thirty acres." That's what I used to call it because whenever we'd see some place we thought would be good, he'd say, "Yeah, I own thirty acres in there."

Needless to say, we were doing some poaching. At one point, he wanted to move the boat around a levee. He got in the boat by himself and was going along the levee. Jim and I were looking up at the sky for ducks. All of a sudden, we heard him. He was sliding out of the boat, head first, into the water. He went totally under water.

He came up spitting and sputtering. He looked like a big, fat hog in there. We got to laughing at him and he got so damn mad, he almost killed both of us. If he would have found his gun, I'm sure he would have shot us.

Another time, Dee Willard and Dale and I were hunting. The water was high that year, and it was raining this day. We were going to the Sanganois and would get to our blind from there. There's one place there where everybody puts their boat in, but the road to it is under water.

Dale's driving an old pickup that belonged to his son Donnie. Dee's sitting in the middle, and I'm on the outside. I told Dale we couldn't get through the road because it was under water. He just kept going and said, "We'll get through. We'll get through."

About then, the right nose of the truck starts going down because he's gone off the road. The right side is my side. If he goes another foot, I know the truck's going in. He stops and opens his door, which is just about facing the sky now, and wallows out of there. Dee scrambles out, then grabs my hand, and helps me out. I'm really scared because, by this time, my seat is under water.

He's cussing all the way as we're walking back. And he's mad at me! He said, "Why didn't you get out of the truck and walk in front? Then I'd have known where the damn road was!" Like it was my fault.

He got the truck out later and asked me to drive it back to Bath, so I did. It had no brakes at all. I drove that thing all the way back to town with no brakes.

—*Bob (Lobo) Lane*

We had small involvements with Dale at different times. I don't remember a case that involved just him. I knew of the Hamms and thought Dale was the most outgoing of the bunch.

I don't know that I ever arrested Dale. There were never too many arrests made of those fellas. They were pretty hard to catch.

None of them really were bad, compared to the ones that came after. Back in Dale's and my day, it was a half-assed gentleman's agreement between us. If you got me, you got me. If you didn't, then ha, ha!

One of the Hamms, years ago, sat and talked to me on tape and told me how they did things. I think at the time he was mad at the clan. One of the relation had sold his boat or something. He was probably sorry he talked to me afterward.

I used that tape at a number of meetings. I used it without identifying him. He was pretty honest as to how they felt. He said he wanted to die on the river, just wanted to go that way. He talked poetically about the river for someone you wouldn't think was poetically inclined.

One night, he took us back in the Sanganois area. We followed him by the light of his cigarette, it was so dark. At one point he extinguished his cigarette, and we ran right into an outcropping. We couldn't see a thing.

He said, "I just wanted to show you what I could do to you if I wanted to."

—Don Hastings
(Undercover operations,
Illinois Department of
Conservation)

Years ago, we were hunting at a local club, and, well, they didn't know we were hunting on it. Dad said, "We're going to stand right here in the brush for a while. We're not going to shoot." It was about an hour and a half before quitting time.

We stood in the brush and waited. "What are we waiting for?" I asked him.

"I'll tell you when we're gonna hunt," he said.

We stood there and pretty soon here came a guy with some five-gallon buckets. He threw what was in the buckets out into the water. Then he left. Dad heard a motor start up and he said, "OK, now we can hunt." Jack Russell had just fed some ducks, and they'd be coming in any minute.

As a kid growing up, we didn't have a lot of duck ground we could go on and shoot, so we had to shoot where we could shoot. So Dad was a good teacher. He started teaching me when I was very young. I still have all the appropriate poacher memories and the poacher's sixth sense, so to speak.

"What the wardens will do," he told me, "is that when you've got a bunch of ducks around, they'll come up on you when you're calling. So what you do is, right in the middle of a nice bunch of ducks working, stop calling. And listen. Because that's when you'll hear them walking, crack a twig or something, and you know it's time to move on."

Even when I sit in duck blinds today on my own property, I still find myself from time to time stopping my calling and just listening for the sound of that twig cracking.

—*Ron Hamm*

I told this story about when they were throwing dynamite on the water. I told it as I was told it. My friend Tom Egizii, who goes to every bar in the country, tells the story that it happened to my dog. He goes to a hundred bars a day. That's his job. It wasn't me, though. My dog got run over by a car, so they think this was my dog.

What they were doing on Grand Island was, they used to throw dynamite out on the ice to blow holes in it. They'd put the decoys in and then slaughter the ducks, because they're looking for open water. This time, they had their dog in the cab of the truck. Dale Hamm and those guys had the windows down, and they'd take TNT, light it, and slide it on the ice. They lit the first one and watched it slide. But the dog got out of the cab of the truck and made a beeline for it.

At first, the guy who owned the dog said, "Oh, my poor dog." All of a sudden, the dog picked up the dynamite and started heading back. The next thing you know, it was no more "poor dog," it was "If I had a gun, I'd kill that dog."

So they start running. And one guy was going to get in the pickup truck, but the other one was smart and he said, "Let's keep running and try to outrun the dog." The dog was having a little trouble getting off the ice. The dog passed up the pickup truck, still running to the guys, when the dynamite went off.

They found four legs and a tail and it blew out the back window of the truck. That's a true story.

—*Tom Flattery*

and Lies

I went hunting up in South Dakota and I stayed at my cousin's place. He was showing me some old guns he had. He brought out a real old Browning shotgun. I looked at it, wasn't very interested, and gave it back to him.

"You didn't look at it very good, did you?" he said.

I looked it all over again and saw, engraved on the side, "Pete Hamm, Browning, Illinois." That gun had been in South Dakota since the 1960s. All of grandpa's kids had bought him this shotgun in the early 1950s and had his name engraved on it.

I said, "Boy, I'd like to have that." So, I traded him a new Remington 1100 for it. I'm the only one in the family who can say I have Pete Hamm's shotgun. It had been shot so much the barrel was paper thin.

Grandpa was hunting with it down on Anderson Lake, shooting ducks out of season for the market. He had two gunnysacks full of ducks. Pretty soon, the wardens were after him, so he took off running through the timber, carrying his two sacks of ducks and his shotgun and all his shells. The wardens were catching up, so he knew he had to drop something. He figured he could get money from selling the ducks to buy another shotgun, so he dropped that and got away.

A couple days later, there came a knock on his door. "Pete," the warden said, "I've got your shotgun." And he also gave him a ticket for shooting ducks out of season.

The kids thought they were really doing something when they engraved his name on that shotgun. But when he dropped it behind that day, it was kind of like leaving his fingerprints there.

—*Don Hamm*

We were all hunting on Lakewood Hunting Club one morning. Dale was on another ground, poaching. He was killing something and we weren't, so we went over and started hunting with him. It started raining, and we killed quite a few. I just had a young dog. My dog was having a hell of a time swimming. Dale says, "Your goddamn dog can't swim."

He starts throwing a duck out for my dog to swim after. He's kidding me about it. All of a sudden some ducks came in. Everybody grabbed a gun, and he shoots left-handed. He ended up with my gun, and I ended up with his gun. He keeps saying, "Your damn dog can't swim. Your damn dog can't swim."

We get back in and he leaves. We left and moved some decoys, then went over to a slough, and there he was, bailing his boat out. Bailing just as fast as he can because he left the plug out of it.

We jumped in and start bailing it out with him. I looked up and said, "Dale, I'll tell you what. If you don't tell anybody my dog can't swim, I won't tell anybody you left the plug out of your boat."

—*Ernie Hoff*

R onnie and Dad and I went to hunt one day at Central Gun
Club. New club members had just leased it that year. We
were inside visiting with them, and they introduced us to all
the new members.

One of them was the caretaker. They said, "Dale, we
bought our caretaker a high-powered rifle, just to make sure
nobody trespasses."

Dad said, "You better file the front sights off it."

"File the front sights off it?" they said. "Why?"

Dad said, real calm, "So when I shove it up his butt, it
won't hurt him so bad."

—*Don Hamm*

He had an old Sea King motor. I knew it wouldn't run. The first time he pulled on the starter, I expected the rope to come off in his hand.

We got in this little, old jonboat. The motor started, and out through the stumps we went. Up over the stumps, one thing and another. No life jackets.

He got us out to the Illinois River. I said, "Dale, we won't ever make it across that river in this." By golly, he got us to the other side in that boat. We commandeered a pickup truck. It was one of his brother's.

About ten o'clock that night we got home. If you would have seen the boat and motor we left there in, you wouldn't ride in it. I mean, you would not ride in it.

—*Jim Gibbs*

Dale and I went out with a third guy to his blind one morning. I started getting suspicious when he started dropping ducks that were about a half-mile away.

I looked down on the floor of the blind and there was a box of lead shot. You can only shoot steel shot now, you know. Lead's illegal. I said, "Dale," and pointed to that box of lead, "what's that?"

He looks at it and says, "Why them dirty sons a bitches. Somebody's been shooting lead in this blind!"

—*Mark Clark*

He called me once and said, "We're going hunting tomorrow. Meet me at Wimpyville."

We met him there, and we were at some cabin there. He had a blind built on his boat and had a motor he borrowed from one of the state conservation guys. We took off down the slough, and Lobo Lane is sitting on a gas tank. I'm in the front of the boat. He told me to shine a flashlight on a riverbank and don't take it off. Don't move the flashlight, he said.

He takes off. This is a 40-horse or 50-horse motor. It's dark as hell. We're talking 4:30 in the morning, something like that. He can't see. The blind's 4-foot-5, and Dale's 4-foot-4. We're going down the slough and I've got the flashlight shining on one bank. Every once in a while I see a stump in the water and I'm trying to point it out to him. Every time I moved that flashlight, he'd just yell at me like crazy. We'd hit a stump and go right over it.

We finally got out in the open water. I'd turned around a couple of times to look at Lobo, and his eyes were THIS big. He's sitting on a gas tank like a bucking bronc.

—*Dee Willard*

Dad called me in about 1986 one Wednesday night and said, "Can you get away tomorrow?" I said I didn't know whether I could or not, and why would I want to?

He said, "I think we can kill some ducks up in the head of Crane Lake. Get down here in the morning, and we'll have some breakfast and go hunting." I said I'd be there.

So I got down there on a Thursday morning. It was getting almost daylight, and we were still eating breakfast. I thought, what the hell are we doing? The old man has finally gone over the hill. He's too old for this anymore. Finally, he said, "OK, it's time for us to go." We went down past the state check station at the Sanganois, got down the gravel road about two miles and he pulled over right alongside the road. Right by a big sign that said No Trespassing.

We stepped out, went to our right through a bunch of trees. The first thing I know, we're wading in water up to our ankles. Then it got up to our knees. He said, "This is where we're gonna shoot." We were standing in a bunch of trees, no decoys, nothing. We'd been there about ten minutes, and here came the ducks. Dad said, "Let's just pick drakes."

So we stood there and started shooting. I expect we had about eighteen drakes down. Dad said, "Let's shoot one more." About that time I raised up and I shot. I didn't hear a second shot, but I saw two ducks falling out of the air. They weren't close together, so I knew I didn't make a double. He shot at the same time. Two mallard drakes hit the water at the same time. We picked up and headed out.

But we took just enough ducks out each trip so that we were legal each time. We took them to a high sand ridge that was about a mile from the state check station. We got them on the ridge, then loaded them all up, and away we went. We knew we were safe.

We hadn't gone a mile when we met the conservation officer. We had twenty ducks in our car. Dad just waved to him and went right off. We'd spent all that time being so careful, and then as soon as we got all our ducks together, there was the officer.

I left the Peoria County state's attorney's office in about 1971, and it was after that, sometime in 1972 or 1973, I was talking to an undercover officer with the state who was working drug cases at the time. She had initially started as a conservation officer. She told me that in their training sessions at the Department of Conservation, they were instructed that if they came upon a boat that had a Hamm in it, they were to check it very carefully. That was part of the training of the Department of Conservation for the state of Illinois.

—*Ron Hamm*

I used to pick ducks by the gunnysacks full. I used to pick them all. I never saw Dale pick one. Jiminy Christmas, it took me a long time. I wouldn't pick a duck now for anything.

Dale's sister used to pick ducks for ten cents a duck. Then they'd hang them by the neck on a clothesline so they'd freeze, and they'd be up high where the cats couldn't get them.

I didn't approve of him killing things outside the law. You've got to go by the law. The poor game wardens didn't have a chance. They were just doing their job.

Dale used to coon hunt a lot, and I'd go with him. I'd hold the flashlight for him while he killed the coon out of a tree.

That day he was arrested and led away in chains, we had to go down to jail and get him out. It was a Sunday, I remember. That's the first time I'd ever seen anybody behind bars. It was horrible.

One day, I looked out our front door and saw a police car and a policeman coming up the front walk. I thought, "I wonder who they're after now?" The officer just wanted to know where somebody in the neighborhood lived. I guess I got plumb paranoid.

I saw Dale last Thanksgiving. We were at Don's house for dinner. I said to Dale, "Do you want a piece of pie?" He said, "You didn't poison it, did you?" I said no, and we got a good laugh over it.

I never did believe in market hunting, but I know he sure had fun when he was doing it.

—*Bernice Oest* (Dale's first wife)

E P I L O G U E

Dale, who turned eighty years old in August 1996, and his wife, Betty, spend their winters in Florida, where Dale helps deplete the state's catfish population. He comes back to Bath in April or May and keeps catfishing every day. While he's fishing, Betty paints. Bath is such a small town, she says, it's good to have a hobby and stay busy. Her subjects, as should come as no surprise, are usually ducks and geese.

A few weeks before the start of the 1993 duck season, Dale and I took a drive near the Sanganois Conservation Area. We were on our way to look at his blinds on Stewart Lake. His son Ron is still an attorney and was assistant state's attorney in Peoria for Peoria County. He started buying the lake about ten years ago. He owns most of it now, and it's prime duck-hunting area. Dale calls it "the duck ground."

Dale had a tough summer in 1993, battling prostate cancer and going back and forth from his home in Bath to the Veterans Administration Hospital in Iowa City. The doctors operated on him and said they had removed the cancer, and it shouldn't be a danger to him, but the fight had left him weak.

It had been a wet summer in central Illinois, and many of the fields along the road were still flooded. We were the first car on the road that morning, and it was lucky that we were. As we drove next to the flooded fields, we kicked up a good number of ducks.

"By God," Dale said, "look at those sons of bitches. Sprigs." By that he means pintails. "I can see them out there splashing, too."

Off to the north, we saw a great cloud of ducks over the trees. We were both excited.

"By God," he said again, "this is just what I needed to see. I didn't think they'd get my blood circulating again but, damn it, this is just what I needed."

As duck season neared, he got stronger. Good thing, too, because there is always a long line of people waiting to hunt with him. He made it out there most mornings during the season. Then, with a few days to go, his wife, Betty talked him into leaving for Florida.

I hunted with him the day before he left. It was one of those raw days when they were going to fly all day. We shot our ducks, but not over the limit. He doesn't do that any-more—at least not very often. When we weren't shooting, we were laughing. The floor of the blind was slick with mud and water, and I slipped once and nearly fell. He got a big kick out of that.

Dale doesn't pick up his ducks until he's ready to go in. "Sure as you're out there picking up a duck," he says, "you'll miss a bunch that would have come in if they hadn't seen you."

He judges where the birds will float until they get hung up in the flooded willow trees. He'll check them out now and then to see that they're still there. Then, when the hunt's over, we go busting through the trees in the boat and find the ducks. This day, we got in my boat to go pick them up. Dale handled the motor and gave me a pretty rough ride in more ways than one. But, strangely enough, getting cussed out by Dale is an honor.

"You got your damn motor locked down," he yelled. "Never, never lock your motor down. If you hit a sunken log, it'll tear the transom right off your damn boat. You dumb son of a bitch.

"Here! Get your gun barrel in the boat. Damn it, get that gun barrel in the boat. Don't leave your gun hanging out like that! We hit a tree (and we hit plenty of them), the branches'll pull that gun right into the water. Don't you know anything? My God, I'll make a duck hunter out of you yet."

The 1994 and 1995 duck-hunting seasons were disappointing. Both years, Dale became disgusted and left for Florida before the season ended. We started with low water both seasons, which meant we couldn't get our blinds out until after the season was under way. There was no way to get a boat on Stewart Lake when it only had two or three inches of water.

In 1994, the weather during the season turned warm and sunny. That meant the ducks stayed north. But in 1995, it was the opposite—bitter cold. That froze what little water there was, and the ducks flew south.

We spent too many days in our blinds just looking at the sky. One morning, when we weren't shooting anything, Dale looked at me and said "If I though it'd do any good. I'd get down on my knees and pray for some ducks. A season like this don't bother you so much," he said, "you've got plenty of duck seasons ahead of you. But me, I don't have many left. I don't like to waste one like this."

In the fall of 1995, we hunted together only once. Dale was seventy-nine then and had a little trouble getting from the boat into the blind. Of course, when I tried to help him in he barked, "Get away. I don't need any help." I knew that was coming.

He had just gotten over a bout with pneumonia and was

finally feeling well enough to hunt. I noted that the temperature was around 40 degrees, and Dale didn't have a coat on. I mentioned it to him, and he said he had two coats in his car but didn't think he'd need them.

"I'm fine," he said, "it's not even cold." As the morning wore on and we didn't do much shooting, he volunteered that he just wasn't going to hunt anymore.

"I'm done after today," he said.

"You mean for the season or for good?" I asked.

"For good," he said.

I told his son Ron about that comment. Ron laughed. "Wait until next fall when we're building blinds, and the ducks are flying, he said. "We'll see whether he's done or not."

If when the autumn chill comes, and the first group of mallards flies over Bath, I'll be very surprised if, as Dale says, they don't get his blood circulating again.

David Bakke

DAVID BAKKE, a recipient of the Penney-Missouri feature-writing award, began his daily newspaper career at the *Sioux City Journal,* moving on to the *State Journal-Register* in Springfield, Illinois, where he was a feature writer and weekly columnist before being named coordinator of *Heartland,* the newspaper's weekly feature magazine. Currently, Bakke is the editor of the *Catholic Times*—the newspaper for the Springfield, Illinois, diocese—which under his editorship has been honored numerous times for general excellence by the National Catholic Press Association.

A Note on the Type

The Last of the Market Hunters was set in Perpetua, a type designed by the controversial designer and social critic Eric Gill and first cut into type by the Monotype Corporation in 1930, about the time that the Hamm boys were beginning to hunt ducks. Gill learned the craft of type design from cutting letters in stone, and the fine serifs of Perpetua are evidence of this work. The book was designed by Gary Gore.